A Primer on Consumer Behavior

A Primer on Consumer Behavior

A Guide for Managers

David W. Stewart

BUSINESS EXPERT PRESS

A Primer on Consumer Behavior: A Guide for Managers

First published in 2018 by
Business Expert Press, LLC
222 East 46th Street, New York, NY 10017
www.businessexpertpress.com

ISBN-13: 978-1-94744-120-0 (paperback)
ISBN-13: 978-1-94744-121-7 (e-book)

Business Expert Press Consumer Behavior Collection

Collection ISSN: 2163-9477 (print)
Collection ISSN: 2163-937X (electronic)

Cover and interior design by Exeter Premedia Services Private Ltd., Chennai, India

First edition: 2018

10 9 8 7 6 5 4 3 2 1

Printed in the United States of America.

Abstract

At its most fundamental level, marketing is about influencing the decision making and behavior of customers. Profitable businesses are built on an understanding of their customers and the creation and delivery of products and services that meet the needs of these customers. This book provides an introduction to consumer and buyer behavior and the many factors that influence consumer behavior, and ultimately, market demand. It is also about how marketers can influence individual customers and market demand. Depending on the particular business, customers may be individuals, households, or organizations. How these individuals and entities make decisions and behave in the market may vary considerably, but an understanding of the factors that influence buyer's decision making and behavior is critical to the marketing and business success of every organization. It has been estimated that 80 percent of all new products fail in the market. The most frequent reason for such failure is a lack of understanding of the needs and behavior of potential customers.

The discipline of consumer research is very mature and there are many comprehensive textbooks and reference books for readers seeking detail. This book is intended to provide a quick, highly accessible introduction to key issues and concepts necessary for understanding market demand and for creating successful marketing programs. The focus of the book is on information likely to be most useful to a practicing manager rather than the student or scholar who is seeking a deep understanding of consumer behavior. For this reason, the book includes "points to ponder" that link basic concepts to marketing practice. The final chapters of the book also point the reader to a variety of additional resources for learning more about consumer behavior in general and consumers in specific markets.

Consumer and buyer behavior includes many different types of activities from recognizing the need for a product, to obtaining information, to the actual purchase decision, to product use, and ultimately to product disposal. Such behavior is rarely, if ever, irrational. Rather, consumers are highly purposeful and the behavior of consumers can readily be understood in the context of the goals consumers pursue and the resources and constraints that consumers confront in pursuit of their goals. While such understanding does not guarantee the success of products, services, and marketing programs, it does dramatically increase the probability of success. This book is a primer on consumer behavior and how knowledge of that behavior contributes to organizational success.

Keywords

buyer behavior, consumers, consumer behavior, demand analysis, drivers of demand, psychology of markets, purchase process

Contents

Preface

Understanding consumer behavior, or customer behavior, is fundamental to business success. Without knowledge of what customers value and why, how customers perceive competitive alternatives, where customers want to buy their products and services, how customers want to pay, and what information will influence customers to purchase, the marketing manager and the business he or she represents is going to market without the vision required for market success. Sometimes, blind luck can lead to success, but more often an absence of knowledge about customers is a recipe for failure, or at minimum, sub-optimal performance. Failure is an especially likely outcome when a firm's competitors have an understanding of customers that the firm does not. This book is intended to provide marketing managers, sales personnel, business owners, and others who make decisions about market offerings a quick, readable introduction to consumer behavior. It is a starting point for identifying questions that every marketing manager should ask about customers.

The good news is that there is an enormous body of literature regarding consumer behavior that has been accumulated over the past century of modern marketing practice and research. There is academic literature, government reports and statistics, and studies by consultants, trade organizations, and research firms. This literature covers broad market trends and consumption patterns, individual product and service markets, basic psychological and social processes that influence consumers, and the competitive dynamics of markets to which consumers respond. This literature is global in scope, reflecting the diversity and opportunities in a global economy.

The volume of literature and information about consumers is also a problem, especially for practicing managers who need to quickly learn about the customers they plan to serve. Multiple courses on consumer behavior often exist in university offerings, and these courses are often taught as social science courses rather than focus on the information needs of practicing or future managers. The many textbooks on consumer behavior are hundreds of pages in length, and like the courses they serve, are often written with a focus on principles of psychology and economics rather than marketing practice. The accumulation of a large and rich body of knowledge about consumers demonstrates that the field has matured and established a strong scientific foundation. Managers are fortunate to be able to build on this body of knowledge. At the same time, the daunting nature of this accumulated literature discourages efforts to master it by busy managers and makes it difficult for managers to find information relevant to their immediate needs in practice.

This book is intended to fill this gap. It is intended to provide a quick read, an overview of important issues, and a discussion of the questions managers should ask about their customers. The title of the book is deliberate; it is designed as a primer. It will not and cannot answer very specific questions about the behavior of customers in very specialized markets defined by particular products or services, in specific geographic locations, at a given moment in time. What it does attempt to do is identify questions every manager should be able to answer about his or her customers. It also provides some initial direction about the answers to those questions and how to obtain answers.

Managers have an important ally for learning about customers—customers themselves. Every manager, whether in a small business or a large corporation is able to find customers and have a conversation. Some large organizations can expend large sums of money and considerable time on conducting formal research on customers. Such studies can be very useful, and if done well, can provide more precise answers than might be obtained using less expensive and less formal research methods. But, every manager has the ability to ask questions of customers, or potential customers, and often, such direct contact and questioning can reveal insights not readily obtained with expensive standardized research methods.

An underlying premise of this book is that consumers are purposive actors in markets who have reasons for behaving as they do. Most customers will share those purposes and reasons if asked. What makes marketing and the study of consumer behavior exciting and interesting, and what creates business opportunity, is the fact that not all consumers are alike. Different customers buying the same product or service may do so for very different purposes and different reasons. Recognition of such diversity requires immersion in the market, appreciation of the role a product or service plays in the life of a consumer, and a willingness to take the time to understand the world of the customer. This volume is intended to as a starting place for this journey of exploration.

The objectives of this primer are straight-forward. After reading this book the reader should come away with an understanding that:

1. Consumers and buyers are purposeful. Understanding and influencing consumer and buyer behavior requires an understanding the goals consumers are pursuing and the problems they are trying to solve when purchasing and using products and services;

2. Consumer and buyer behavior are complex and influenced by many environmental and psychological characteristics and processes. This complexity gives rise to differences among customers even within the same market and even within the same consumer at different points in time;

3. Environmental factors that influence consumer and buyer behavior include economic, social, demographic, competitive, and situational influences. These factors are "drivers" of demand, that is, they give rise to reasons customers buy or don't buy. They are also the reasons that consumers change over time;

4. Psychological characteristics and processes that influences on consumer and buyer behavior include motivation, emotion, perception, learning, memory, attitude, and personality. Success requires understanding the psychology of customers;

5. Consumers and buyers use a variety of different decision-making strategies and decision rules to reduce the effort required by shopping and to arrive at decisions about product and service alternatives. Ultimately, marketing is about influencing decisions; influence requires knowledge;

6. Consumer and buyer satisfaction are also influenced by many factors. Satisfaction plays a key role in future purchases and brand loyalty. Understanding how to satisfy customers and keep them coming back to purchase again is a key to business success;

7. Organizations are also buyers of products and services. A key element for understanding organizational purchasing is the identification of

the buying center, that is, the individuals who are involved in one role or another in the purchase process. Ultimately, even purchases by organizations are made by people whose motivations and incentives need to be understood; and

8. There are many places to obtain information about customers ranging from simple face-to-face conversations to highly sophisticated research methods. There is a never an obstacle to learning about customers even if resource and time constraints limit the use of some sources and methods.

Business success starts with a deep understanding of customers. This primer is intended as a starting point for the development of such understanding.

Acknowledgments

This book, like all books, is the result of an accumulation of experiences. I wish to acknowledge my teachers, students, colleagues, and consulting clients who have presented me with interesting questions and opportunities to interact with and learn about a rich array of consumers in hundreds of market contexts. I also wish to acknowledge the many, many consumers who have shared their views, behaviors, and sometimes the most intimate details of the lives with me during my quest to learn about them.

I owe a special debt of gratitude to Rajiv Grover and Naresh Malhotra who initially encouraged me to develop a chapter on consumer behavior for a book on marketing management. Naresh also encouraged me to turn that chapter into a short, managerially focused book.

While I take responsibility for content of the book I had help in its completion. Christina Faulkner of Loyola Marymount University was instrumental in tracking down and obtaining permissions for use of the items reproduced from other sources. The publisher of the book, Business Expert Press, was very helpful in making my words become a book.

Finally, I thank my wife of more than 40 years, Lenora, who has tolerated my time studying other people and who has been my decades long partner in co-consumption.

CHAPTER 1

Consumer Behavior: The Foundation of Marketing

This chapter provides an introduction to consumer and buyer behavior. We will generally use the term consumer behavior to refer to the activities of individual consumers and households and use the term buyer behavior to refer to the purchasing activities of organizations. It is important to note that consumer and buyer behavior includes many different types of activities from recognizing the need for a product or service, to obtaining information, to the actual purchase decision, to product use, and ultimately to product disposal.

At its most fundamental level, marketing is about influencing the decision-making and behavior of customers. Depending on the particular business, customers may be individuals, households, or organizations and how they make decisions may vary considerably. An understanding of the factors that influence buyer's decision-making and behavior is critical to marketing and business success.

For example, an understanding of the alternative uses consumers made of its product allowed Arm and Hammer to revitalize a mature baking product into a cleaner and deodorizer that is now purchased as a carpet cleaner; a deodorizer for refrigerators, sinks, garbage cans, and cat litter; laundry detergent; and toothpaste, among others. The success of Arm and Hammer stands in sharp contrast to many companies. It has been estimated that 80 percent of all new products fail in the market.[1] The most frequent reason for such failure is a lack of understanding of customers and potential customers.

Consumers Are Purposeful

The fundamental organizing principle of consumer and buyer behavior is that buyers purchase and use products and services in pursuit of goals. Buyer's purchases and uses of products and services are neither random nor irrational. Although not always apparent to an observer, consumers behave in a systematic manner that can be understood in the context of goal pursuit. The key is discovering such underlying motivation.

For example, what may appear to be random switching from brand to brand by a consumer may, in fact, be a systematic effort to evaluate brands (or recent improvements in brands). On the other hand, another consumer who regularly switches brands may be seeking variety and yet another consumer may be seeking the brand that is being promoted with the lowest price. All three of these consumers appear similar in their brand-switching behavior but what they buy on any purchase occasion may be quite different. What appears to be inexplicable and even random behavior is readily explained once the motives of these consumers are understood.[2]

Point to Ponder

Some products can serve multiple purposes. For example, Jell-O can be used in a salad or as a dessert; Bisquick can be used to make pancakes and biscuits. What other products can you identify that have multiple and varied uses? Do the same consumers use them for different purposes or do different consumers use them differently? How would the answer to the latter question influence marketing decisions?

It is often useful to think of consumers as bundles of goals and use occasions.[3] Consumers have particular sets of purposes for which they buy and use products and services. These goals change as the circumstances of the consumer change. They change with the consumer's age, education, and occupation. They change over the course of the family life cycle. And they change from one social situation to another. Understanding goals and how they differ from buyer to buyer and how they change over time for the same buyer are important elements in product design, service delivery, and marketing planning.

Understanding Consumer's Goals

Consumers use products for many purposes; it is not always apparent which purposes are served by which products. Beer may be consumed because it quenches thirst, but it may also be closely linked to social situations in which the consumer wishes to feel accepted and a part of the group. Indeed, there is evidence that many consumers consumer different alcoholic beverages and drink brands depending on situational factors.[4] While any brand of beer may satisfy thirst, not all beers are equally acceptable in social situations. Thus, an inexpensive generic beer is fine for home consumption, but a premium brand may be preferred in social situations.[5]

Discovering the linkages between products and brands and specific consumer goals is a difficult task. One approach to identifying these linkages has been referred to as means-end analysis, or laddering.[6] Means-end analysis focuses on the linkages between:

- the attributes that exist in products (the "means"),
- the consequences for the consumer provided by the attributes, and
- the goals (the "ends") these consequences serve or reinforce.

Means-end analysis is generally carried out by means of an in-depth, one-on-one interview technique that attempts by asking successive questions to uncover the relationship of products to basic values. For example, in one application of the technique a relationship preference for a particular flavored snack chip and self-esteem was uncovered.[7] Such a relationship is not immediately obvious but took the following form:

The discovery of such linkages provides a number of opportunities for marketing activities. The marketer might emphasize the linkage between the chip and self-esteem by actually playing out the value chain in a commercial or the marketer might select any one link as a point of emphasis in an advertisement, such as emphasizing a feeling of satisfaction after consuming only a few chips. Alternatively, the marketer might focus on further enhancement of the chip's flavor to increase satisfaction after eating only a few chips. Yet another action might be reducing calories in the chips and communicating to consumers that they can eat more without fear of gaining weight.

Figure 1.1 provides an illustration of an advertisement that links a specific benefit to a product. In this advertisement for La-Z-Boy there is an explicit association of comfort with the chair and sofa, and it is the comfort benefit that is the focus of the advertisement.

Figure 1.1 Products are a means to an end

Point to Ponder

Think about participation in a very public charitable event, such as the challenge for charity, the MBA charity event, or some similar affair. Develop the likely means-ends chains for those MBA students who might participate. What do these several chains suggest about how you might go about motivating participation?

While goals provide a powerful organizing framework for describing and explaining consumer's decision-making and behavior, goals exist within a broader context. Characteristics of the individual and of the social and environmental context influence the development and enactment of consumer's goals.[8] A consumer's goals in turn define, at least in part, the individual's personality and sense of self, and influence the more proximate social and environmental conditions within which the consumer makes decisions and uses products, because the consumer's goals also direct decisions about where the consumer will spend his or her time. Thus, while consumer's goals represent the reasons for a purchase, the enactment of those goals is influenced by many other factors. These factors will be explored in subsequent chapters.

Takeaways

As a marketer, the most fundamental goal is to influence how consumers (individuals) and buyers (organizations) make decisions. To achieve this end, it is paramount that a marketer understands people making buying decisions are pursuing specific goals. These goals may change over time, they may vary from one situation to another, but they always exist. Discovery of these motives is the starting place for understanding and insight. By recognizing how they vary from buyer to buyer and how they evolve over time, the marketer can make informed, confident, and impactful decisions about market offerings, branding and marketing strategies. These goals of a consumer are the product of the consumer's individual personality. It is this personality that determines where they spend time, who they trust, when they buy, and what they buy. Throughout this book, we will explore these links and what they say about the greater context of personality to better understand and develop strategies around consumer behavior.

Notes

1. Wagner (2013).
2. Bagozzi and Dholakia (1999, pp. 19–32).
3. Ratneshwar et al. (2001, pp. 147–57).
4. Social Issues Research Centre (2018).
5. Temporal (2001, pp. 170–80).
6. Thomas and Olson (2001); Gutman (1982, pp. 60–72).
7. Gutman (1997, pp. 545–60); Thomas and Gutman (1988, pp. 11–31).
8. Ratneshwar, Mick, and Huffman (2003).

CHAPTER 2

Forces Influencing Buyer Decision Making and Behavior

Chapter 1 introduced the importance of understanding consumers' goals as drivers of consumer behavior. Consumers' goals arise from many sources and are influenced by numerous factors. This chapter explores the factors that influence consumers' goals.

In late 2015, clothing retailer Nordstrom released a holiday sweater intended to appeal to their Jewish customers. The Hanukkah-themed sweater featured holiday-appropriate symbols but the message of the shirt "Chai Maintenance" (loosely pronounced "High Maintenance") and "J.A.P." (Jewish American Princess) played upon common, derogatory stereotypes of Jewish-American women that may be considered "okay" in family and small community settings but were certainly off limits for a national retailer. By not evaluating the various forces influencing the consumer's decision beyond religious or ethnic affiliation, they ended up with a product that they were quickly forced to pull from their shelves due to backlash from the consumers they intended to target as well as a public relations nightmare.

Buyers are acted upon by many forces, some originating in the past, some originating in the present, and some based on future expectations. Figure 2.1 illustrates this point. The inner circle in the diagram represents the person and his or her personality and portfolio of goals. The individual has certain needs and goals—some physiological in origin, some acquired through learning—and a history of past experiences, many of which can no longer be recalled consciously, but which have been internalized in the present personality structure.

In addition, the person has hopes, expectations, and fears of the future. Thus, the past, present, and future exist simultaneously as forces influencing behavior. The area surrounding the person is the environment in which he or she acts. It also contains forces that act upon him or her—forces that are physical, social, and economic in nature.

The specific context in which buyer behavior occurs is the market. Indeed, what differentiates the study of buyer behavior from other disciplines that study human behavior is this market context. Figure 2.2 provides a more detailed illustration of the factors and processes that influence buyers. There are many idiosyncratic factors that may influence buyer behavior, but among the more general factors that influence all buyers in one way or another are:

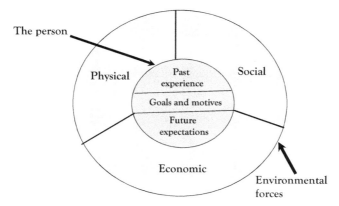

Figure 2.1 Forces acting on the buyer

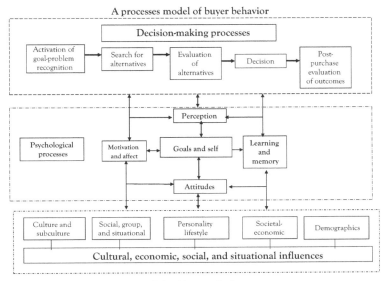

Figure 2.2 A processes model of buyer behavior

- Cultural and subcultural factors
- Social, group, and situational factors
- Personality and lifestyle
- Societal and economic factors
- Demographic factors

Cultural and Subcultural Influences

Thorstein Veblen is generally considered the pioneer of "cultural determination" in human behavior, which addresses the role culture in consumers' purchases. His first major work, *The Theory of the Leisure Class*, was a theory of consumption.[1] Veblen's premise is that goals or needs do not result from some indefinable, subjective feeling on the part of consumers. Rather, they are a social phenomenon, the product of social conditioning. Such social conditioning may be more immediate and unique to an individual or it can be the result of generations of social interaction that produces shared values and prescriptions for behavior. It is this long-term social interaction and its results that are collectively called culture.

Culture affects most of what we do. The fact that men in the United States wear pants rather than robes or gowns is culturally determined.

The staples of our diet; our methods of food preparation and service; the roles of males and females in the home and in society; our customs of sleeping in beds, sitting in chairs, the emphasis on punctuality, the glorification of competition, and the pattern of working to acquire material possessions we do not have time to enjoy—all are manifestations of a cultural inheritance.

Point to Ponder

How important is culture? What purpose does culture serve? Will it disappear as the world economy becomes more integrated? Think of several products or services that will vary with respect to their cultural significance, i.e., how they might be perceived differently as a result of cultural differences.

Few societies are so homogeneous that everyone shares all of the same cultural values. Rather, there will be some groups of people who for reasons of history, geography, or other circumstances share some values with the dominant culture but differ in important ways. Such groups are referred to as *subcultures*. They may share many of the values of the dominant culture, or they may share relatively few.[2] Marketers often define subcultures in terms of ethnicity, age, geography, race, religion, lifestyle, and even political ideology, though such "subcultures" may not meet the technical requirements of a precise definition. Among ethnic groups, the two largest in the United States are Blacks and those of Hispanic descent but there are many others including Asian-Americans, of which there are many varieties, and Native Americans, among others. These groups

---

Point to Ponder

Being younger, a member of an ethnic group, or even a follower of a particular religious belief could make you a member of a subculture. Are you a member of a "subculture?" Do you think of yourself in these terms? Why or why not? Does your identification depend on the situation or context? How helpful is this type of classification for marketing?

---

often share similar values, food preferences, grooming needs, and other characteristics that require special appeals, products, and services. In terms of age, teenagers and mature consumers are most often identified as special markets.

Social, Group, and Situational Influences

Groups are the fundamental units of a social system. They function to promote survival, carry out work, achieve goals, provide solace and comfort for the individual, and entertain and relax their members. An enormous amount of consumer and buyer behavior occurs in the context of and often for a group. The key to understanding the influence of groups on consumer and buyer behavior is the extent to which the individual looks to a group for information about how to behave. Groups that help define appropriate behavior for members and would-be members are called *reference groups*, and they are very important for marketing. Family, school groups, church, and professional organizations are all reference groups. Fraternities and sororities are reference groups. So is the group of friends that goes out together every Saturday night.

There are two general ways in which reference groups influence consumer behavior—through normative social influence and through informational social influence. Normative social influence involves an individual conforming to the expectations of the group. Informational social influence involves group members providing information that influences the behavior of the individual.

Point to Ponder

What are your reference groups? How do they influence your buying behavior? How would a marketer use your reference groups to influence your purchasing behavior?

The Family as a Consuming Unit

One of the most important types of social groups both within society as a whole and for understanding buyer behavior is the family. In marketing, we often talk about decision making as though it were always an individual process, whereas many product and service purchase decisions are group decisions in which all family members have a voice. The subjects of family decisions range from automobiles to vacations, with the patterns of influence varying from product to product. When we consider that two-thirds of all U.S. households are family units,[3] we must recognize that an understanding of family decision patterns is essential for the successful marketing of many products and services. In contemporary society, families can take many forms, but they remain an important unit for purchasing and consumption. In recognition of the varieties of family units, The families project by Betty Crocker celebrated the many faces and structures of modern families (https://youtube.com/watch?v=ukg3Kj7-hSI).

Point to Ponder

If you do not have a child, visit the local grocery store (if you have a child you get credit for experience and can do this exercise from memory). Find the following products and where they are located in the store: Pedialyte, ketchup (any brand), and breakfast cereal. For each of these products indicate how you think a child influences the decision, the nature of this influence, and how marketing actions might influence the child. Do you observe anything in the way the products are located and displayed in the store that suggests the influence of children on the purchase decision?

Situational Influences

Many situational factors influence consumer behavior. The otherwise frugal consumer who experiences car trouble in a remote area on a cross country trip may be willing to pay a large premium to have her automobile repaired quickly. An otherwise impulsive shopper may be so insulted by a retail salesperson that he decides not to purchase the item that has struck his fancy.

Such situational influences may seem random, but it is important to recognize that consumers make choices about the situations in which they place themselves. The same consumer that willingly stands in line for a ride at Disneyland may be very impatient standing in line at the local grocery store.

Personality and Lifestyle

Personality is widely recognized by psychologists and laypersons alike as a fundamental component of human behavior. People develop distinct "personalities," which are simply tendencies to behave in a consistent fashion over time and across occasions. Even though a consumer's score on an introversion scale may have little to do with what brand of detergent the consumer buys, the introverted consumer might prefer to avoid in-store shopping while embracing online shopping. Similarly, a consumer's desire for sensation seeking and risk taking may make that consumer more open to new product ideas than a consumer who is less sensation seeking and more risk aversive.

To improve upon standardized personality inventories developed by psychologists, the successful applications of personality theory to marketing have tended to involve tailor-made measures of personality characteristics that focus on traits specifically related to shopping, decision making, and product use. The use of such tailor-made measures has paved the way for what has become known as *psychographics*, also referred to as *lifestyle and activity, interest and opinion (AIO)* research.

Psychographics is a quantitative research procedure that is especially useful when demographic, socioeconomic, and user/nonuser analyses are not sufficient to explain and predict buyer behavior. More specifically, psychographics provides a means for describing the characteristics of buyers (both individual consumers and even of organizations) that have bearing on their responses to products, packaging, distribution strategies, and marketing communications. Such variables may include a broad range from self-concept and lifestyle, to goals, attitudes, interests, and opinions, as well as perceptions of product characteristics. Psychographic analysis of customers can provide a very rich description of customers. While it is impossible to list all of the questions that might be conceived for inclusion in a psychographic questionnaire, typical questions are shown in Table 2.1.

Table 2.1 Representative psychographic items

Attitudes and Values (Agree or Disagree)
1. Generally speaking, most people are trustworthy and honest.
2. Everything is changing too fast today.
3. My greatest achievements are ahead of me.
4. I believe a woman can work outside the home even if she has small children and still be a good mother.
5. I like to try new and different things.
6. TV is my main form of entertainment.
7. I'm a "spender" rather than a "saver."

Interests and Activities (How Often)
1. Competing in team sports (for example, soccer, baseball, basketball, etc.)
2. Going on a family outing
3. Going out for the evening for drinks and entertainment
4. Going to the movies
5. Visiting art galleries and museums
6. Listening to music
7. Collecting or making something (for example, hobbies)

Opinions and Beliefs (Agree or Disagree)
1. Most public officials are interested in my concerns.
2. U.S. automobile manufacturers produce lower quality vehicles than Japanese manufacturers.
3. Most firms are concerned about how satisfied their customers are.
4. The environment is threatened by modern technology.
5. Genetically modified foods are dangerous.
6. Nuclear power is the answer to our energy needs.
7. There is too much violence on television.

There are a number of commercially available psychographic studies. VALS™ (an acronym for value and life styles program), offered by SRI, is perhaps the largest and most comprehensive application of psychographics to marketing.[4] VALS™ has identified nine basic types of consumers based on psychographics: two types of "need-driven" consumers, three types of "outer-directed" consumers, and four types of "inner-directed" consumers. Many organizations have developed their own psychographic profiles. For example, Young and Rubicam have developed what is calls the cross-cultural consumer characterization, or 4C model, which it based on Maslow's hierarchy of needs.[5]

Point to Ponder

Consider the questions in Table 2.1. How could consumers' answers to these types of questions be useful for understanding buyer behavior? In what ways might answers to these questions inform the design of marketing activities? For example, how might knowing that a consumer spends more time visiting art galleries and museums than watching television be used for scheduling advertising and promotions designed to reach that consumer?

Lifestyle segments can be overlaid on geographic information, such as zip code, to profile consumers who live in specific areas. For example, Claritas has identified 68 consumer segments within the United States and provides a description of the most common segments in each zip code area.[6] Such information can be especially helpful when planning the location of a retail business and in targeting marketing communications to specific types of households. Figure 2.3 provides an example of a Claritas profile for one zip code.

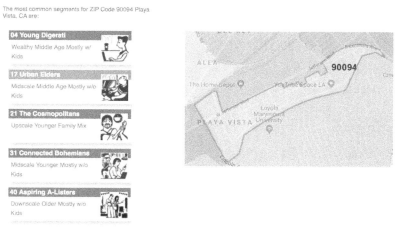

Figure 2.3 Example of Claritas lifestyle segments for 90094 zip code

Source: https://segmentationsolutions.nielsen.com/mybestsegments/Default.jsp?ID=20&menuOption=ziplookup&pageName=ZIP%2BCode%2BLookup&filterstate=&sortby=segment_code&prevSegID=CLA.PZP.

In marketing, personality and lifestyle variables can be used effectively in two ways. First, they can be used as a basis for market segmentation. For example, there are products that appeal to certain personality types. Among fragrance products, perfumes for women and colognes for men, there are strong preferences for particular scents that are associated with personality—fresh and clean; exotic and energetic; youthful; or man or woman-of-the-world? Consider Procter and Gamble's *Old Spice brand*, which appeals to gamers who enjoy *Dungeons and Dragons* by inviting them to download the "Old Spice Gentleman Class"[7] and features a website (http://oldspice.com/) that includes the "The Old Spice School of Swagger." Second, personality and lifestyle variables can be used for devising appeals that activate the interest of consumers. For example, one of the most successful advertising campaigns for liquor products featured "Dewar's Profiles," in which consumers of Dewar's Scotch are featured as a hero and achievers—doers. The use of celebrities as spokespersons for a product is another example of a marketing appeal based on personality. For example, Breitling, the watch company, used John Travolta as a spokesperson for more than a decade. The Breitling advertising not only played on the celebrity of John Travolta, but also emphasized his avocation as a pilot (http://newsmediaworks.com.au/brands-thank-their-lucky-stars-for-standout-ads/).

Societal and Economic Influences

Culture and demography are not the only large-scale phenomena that influence buyer behavior. Changes in the general economy, such as

---

Point to Ponder

Public policy in many countries is designed to influence the long-term demographics of populations. For example, China had a one child per family policy for many years, the United States provides low cost loans for education, and Sweden provides comprehensive childcare for preschool children. What effects do such policies have? What effects would you consider positive? Why? What effects would you consider negative? Why? How do such policies influence buyer behavior?

recession, impact purchasing plans and consumption. Technological changes introduce new products and services and new ways of doing things while simultaneously making other products and services obsolete. Buyers must respond to these changes by replacing products, by learning to do things differently, and by integrating new products and patterns of behavior into their daily routines. For example, during recessions it is very common for consumers to trade down in their selection of restaurants.[8]

Demographic Influences

Demography is the science of populations.[9] It is concerned with describing both the current characteristics of populations and changes taking place within those populations. Among the more common of these characteristics are age, gender, race and ethnic origin, marital status, birth rates, mortality rates, and the geographical dispersion of the population. Patterns of movement of the population, income, education, and occupation are also factors of interest. Individual buyer behavior and the behavior of markets in general are influenced by the composition of the population. Because purchasing patterns are often closely related to demographic characteristics, they provide a useful tool for determining the potential demand for products and services.

Point to Ponder

Assume that gasoline prices were to double overnight as the result of international conflict. How do you think buyers would respond? Buyers include businesses who must pass along costs to individual consumers and individual consumers who must pay the price. How do you think businesses will respond? Will all consumers respond in the same way?

Social Stratification and Social Class

Demographic factors often work together to produce groups of consumers who are similar to one another. One especially relevant composite classification combines income, education, and occupation to define social

Li Yi Model of the Chinese Social Stratification, 2005

Figure 2.4 Changing social class membership in China

Source: Yi, Li (2005), *Structure and Evolution of Chinese Social Stratification*, Lanham, MD: University Press of America.

status or social class. Social class has had a controversial history.[10] It has been widely applied to the study of consumers and market behavior. Social classes should have important implications for marketing. The differences between the readers of *The New Yorker* and *True Confessions* are real, not imaginary. And this phenomenon is not unique to any one country. Social classes exist almost everywhere. Indeed, social classes have emerged in many formally "classless" societies, such as China. Figure 2.4 provides an illustration of the social classes that have emerged in China over the past 50 years and how membership in these classes has changed.[11]

Takeaways

Many forces act upon buyers and consumers. The past, present, and future can all influence decisions. Breaking these forces down into categories helps us take a closer look at these forces and how we may be able to influence them. They include:

- Cultural and subcultural factors
- Social, group, and situational factors
- Personality and lifestyle
- Societal and economic factors
- Demographic factors

Cultural factors include those factors that are directly related to the over-arching culture. We discussed the fact that men in United States usually wear pants rather than a robe because of culture. Subcultures also exist within a given culture. Forces that arise from things like ethnicity, geography, or political affiliation may play upon them as well, influencing buying decisions.

Consumers are also part of various social groups. Groups serve many functions for an individual or organization. Marketers must not only identify these groups, but also how much influence each group has on an entity's decision-making. A specific situation may also influence decision-making. Someone may have no problem paying more when a product or service is perceived as a great convenience to them or it is solving a pressing problem. A customer may be willing to wait for something in one case; in another, they may go with a competitor.

If we stopped at this higher level, we would discount individual tendencies. Personality traits like risk-aversion and adventure-seeking play their part in the process. Psychographic methods quantify personality and help us evaluate the personalities of a target audience, predicting buyer behavior.

Point to Ponder

How do you personally feel about the notion of social class? Do you identify with a social class? Do you think others would place you in a social class? Is social class something marketers should consider in developing their marketing plans?

Economic forces can enter the picture at both a high-level and the individual level. At a societal level, you may have a recession encouraging the multitude to cut back. At a more individual level you may have people in a certain industry facing economic uncertainty because their field of expertise has become obsolete through technological advancements or societal shifts.

Finally, we have demographics factors such as similar age, ethnicity, marital status, geography, and so on. The many combinations of these various factor generate classes of people, who demonstrate similar buying patterns. By understanding these forces and the inter-play among them marketers can develop more effective marketing strategies.

Notes

1. Thorstein (1899, Reprinted 2005).
2. Hoyer, MacInnis, and Pieters (2012).
3. Jonathan, Lewis, and Kreider (2013).
4. Strategic Business Insights (2018).
5. Young and Rubicam (2018); Issuu (2018).
6. Claritas (2108).
7. Old Spice Commercial (2018).
8. Richard (2001).
9. The U.S. Census Bureau provides up-to-date demographic information about the United States and links to information in other countries on its website at: http://census.gov/
10. Wright (2005).
11. Li (2005).

CHAPTER 3

Psychological Processes that Influence Consumer Behavior

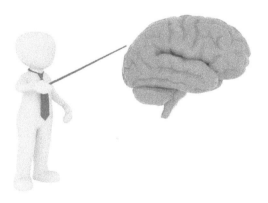

In 1999, GEICO, insurance once reserved for federal employees, quickly became a household name by introducing their fun, informative, and quickly beloved gecko. Playing on words and human emotion, they introduced the GEICO gecko, who pleaded with the public to stop calling him to sign up for insurance and asking them to call GEICO instead. Through clever and memorable advertising, this relatively unknown company quickly became a household name. With a somewhat dry sense of humor and subtle Cockney-accent (in later iterations), this animated character proceeded to travel the United States, recounting his mishaps, adventures, and gratefulness for having car insurance through GEICO, making GEICO the sensible choice to which people felt connected and of which they wanted to be a part.

As we have seen, there are many external factors and individual difference factors that influence buyer behavior. These factors do not

GEICO's First Video Featuring Gecko

https://youtube.com/watch?v=6Qc1H2SMK1s

operate on passive human beings. A variety of psychological processes that are common to all human experience play a critical role in buyer behavior. Buyers are motivated to purchase, experience emotion, perceive and categorize products, learn from experience, and form evaluative judgments about products, people, and companies. Much of the work of marketing is about affecting such basic psychological processes as attention, emotion, perception, formation of beliefs, attitude change, and decision making.

Motivation and Emotion

Motivation refers to the reason or set of reasons that give rise to specific behaviors. It is the process by which goals are established and pursued. As was observed earlier in this chapter, an understanding of the goals of consumers and of the purpose or purposes a product serves for consumers is critical to marketing planning. Motivation and emotion are inextricably linked. One motivation theorist, Reeve, suggests that emotions are the energizing bases for motives.[1] Psychologist Ross Buck suggests that motivation and emotion are manifestations of the same underlying process.[2] Unrealized goals produce feelings, such as longing, hope, and frustration that energize behavior and realized goals produce feelings of joy, satisfaction, and contentment.

Successful marketing activities prompt buyers to action. By appealing to important goals and the emotions associated with achieving or not achieving these goals, the marketer can energize buyers. Holbrook and Hirschman have also noted that a great deal of consumer behavior is directed by the goals of producing specific feelings such as excitement and fun.[3] The pursuit of "feelings" often leads to particular types of consumer behavior, for example, visits to the amusement park, a romantic dinner in an intimate restaurant, travel to new and exotic places, and the purchase of musical recordings.

Point to Ponder

Some of the most memorable television commercials have had strong emotional appeals. Think of recent television commercials that you have seen that have an emotional appeal. How is emotion used in the commercial? Do you think the commercial evokes an emotional response among viewers? Does the emotional response motivate action? If not, what is the purpose of using emotion?

Perception

Perception is the process by which consumers attend, select, obtain, interpret, and organize information. In other words, perception is about how consumers give meaning to the world. Much of the work of the marketer involves efforts to influence the perceptions of consumers. Marketing activities not only involve the provision of information, through such vehicles as advertising, personal selling, websites, and product brochures, but also active efforts to help consumers organize that information. Sometimes aiding perception is a matter of making things visible. Figure 3.1

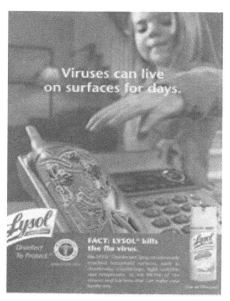

Figure 3.1 Visualizing a problem and its solution

is an example of an advertisement that helps consumers "visualize" a problem and its solution. "Germs" are not readily visible on clothing and surfaces, but advertising for Lysol makes them visible and helps consumers "visualize" a problem and its solution—Lysol Disinfectant Spray, of course (see also https://www.youtube.com/watch?v=BHGBsqOaWmI).

Facilitating the organization of information, a psychological process called perceptual categorization, is one of the marketer's most important jobs. If consumers have trouble categorizing a product in terms of its use, there is little likelihood that they will buy it. A case in point is the different experiences of two food companies in introducing two new products. The two products were similar, almost identical in nature, consisting of a powder to which milk was added to make a delicious, nutritious drink. The company, known as General Foods at the time, called its product "Brim" and advertised it for a variety of purposes: as a nutritious energy drink for children; as a beverage to be drunk with dinner; as a before-bedtime snack; and as a nutritious diet food for those who wanted to lose weight. The brand positioning was ambiguous, consumers had difficulty categorizing Brim in a meaningful way, the test markets were unsuccessful, and eventually the brand was withdrawn from the market.

Later, General Foods used the same brand name for an instant coffee. In contrast, Carnation, now a part of Nestle, called their product "Instant Breakfast," positioning it for people who did not have time to prepare breakfast and nutritionally characterizing it as being the equivalent of a glass of orange juice, a piece of toast, two slices of bacon, and an egg. Instant Breakfast was an outstanding marketing success.

Learning and Memory

Learning may be defined as a process by which behavior capabilities are changed as the result of experience.[4] Such experience can be direct or indirect, formal or informal, and conscious or unconscious. Learning plays an important role in consumer and buyer behavior. With experience, buyers learn what they like and do not like, how to use products, what product attributes meaningfully differentiate products, and even how to shop. Children learn how to become shoppers and consumers and adults confronted with a first time buying decision often spend a great deal of time learning about the category and the characteristics of products. With learning, buyers become more discerning and efficient shoppers.

Learning

Learning is about behavior change. When we have learned something, we are capable of responding differently than before the learning experience, although we may not do so. This aspect of learning is of particular importance to marketing. Most magazine and television advertising is not expected to send the consumer rushing to the store to buy the product. Rather, it is intended to provide information (learning) about the product that eventually will lead to a change in behavior.

Memory

One more outcome of learning and experience is memory. Memory plays a critical role in consumer behavior. For example, a consumer may see a television commercial for a new fast food product. The product sounds appealing and a novel break from typical fast food fare, so she stores the information in memory. A few days later the consumer finds herself in need of a quick lunch and remembers the new product she saw advertised. This memory for the new product leads her to the fast food restaurant where the product is offered and she makes a purchase.

Point to Ponder

Customer satisfaction with a new product, such as a new mobile telephone with increased functionality, often increases over time as the product is used. Why does this occur? What is the role that learning plays in this change in customer satisfaction? Does this role of learning suggest anything about how a marketer might increase customer satisfaction?

Memory is an active process and much of the information in the consumer's environment is not actively processed. For marketers this means that much of the information they are providing to consumers is lost and not committed to memory by consumers. For this reason, repetition is critical to helping consumers commit information to memory. A single advertising exposure is often not enough for consumers to move information from STM to long-term memory. The creation of engaging advertising or compelling sales messages can also encourage consumers to actively process information and thereby facilitate its recall over the longer term. This is also the reason that marketers spend so much effort on attracting the attention of consumers and providing memory aids, like slogans, jingles, and mnemonic devices that facilitate information processing and memory.

Point to Ponder

What devices do marketers use to facilitate and encourage consumers to rehearse information about products and services? If you were to develop the cognitive link for a brand such as Disney or McDonalds, what do you think would be included? What would the links for a lesser known brand, like Nestle's Buitoni brand of pasta, include? Can you infer anything about the strength or value of a brand from the richness of its associations?

Information in memory may be organized in different ways by different consumers. The way in which information is stored in memory can have a profound effect on consumer behavior because the organization of products in memory represents the way in which the consumer thinks about a product market. Consider what happens when a consumer first categorizes the pain reliever category into aspirin and non-aspirin subcategories. When products are categorized in this way Bayer and Tylenol are never considered as direct competitors. If the consumer first selects a non-aspirin pain reliever, Bayer is not considered. On the other hand, if the consumer does not first categorize pain relievers as non-aspirin and aspirin, but regards all as simply pain relievers, Bayer and Tylenol are direct competitors. The way in which consumers think about a market has been called product partitioning and the set of associations for a particular brand is its position or image in the market.

In one classic Tylenol commercial (https://www.youtube.com/watch?v=h_ijcs5PGQ4) the company focuses on the relief of fever among children and contrasts Tylenol with aspirin. It also informs viewers that Tylenol is recommended by more pediatricians, which is another source of differentiation, as well as an appeal based on the credibility of experts and authority figures, pediatricians.

The implications of such brand positioning are profound. Consumers frequently use brand names as a general descriptor for a given product offering. As a result, individual attribute information may be lost. For example, consider the following brand names commonly used as general product descriptors among some consumers:

Frisbee = throwable disc
Pop Tarts = toaster pastries
Lysol = disinfectant spray
Q-tip = cotton swab
Kleenex = tissue
Tylenol = non-aspirin pain reliever
Coke = soft drink (in the Southern U.S.)

There is, in fact, evidence that as consumers become more familiar with a product category, they tend to do more processing by brand rather than by attributes of brands and make more global evaluations of brands.[5] This often makes it difficult to change beliefs and attitudes toward familiar brands since consumers have ceased to consider their individual attributes. Even a significant change in a familiar product may fail to alter perceptions of the product if consumers are responding to the brand name rather than its individual attributes.

Forgetting

Closely related to the concepts of learning and memory is the concept of forgetting. Forgetting is a process whereby some response, skill, or cognitive material is extinguished or lost. There is a common notion that forgetting occurs as the result of the passage of time. In fact, there is no evidence to suggest that the mere passage of time causes forgetting or extinction. Rather, forgetting appears to be an active process of unlearning or the learning of new responses or skills that interfere with the memory for older skills and responses.[6] Interference is a common phenomenon. When someone is required to learn different responses to similar stimuli—for example, two ads for competing products—learning of the second response interferes with the retention of the original response.[7] In general, the greater the similarity of stimuli, the greater the interference will be. This is one reason why marketers seek to design unique products, and advertisers try to create novel advertisements. The more distinctive the product or ad (the less similar to other products or ads), the less likely interference will occur.

Point to Ponder

What does "interference" suggest about the influence of competitors' marketing activities? How might such interference be reduced by the marketer?

The Role of Attitudes

Another important psychological process is the formation of attitudes. It is frequently the case that learning is accompanied by an evaluative process that results in consumers' forming positive or negative feelings. Most decisions that buyers make are preceded by an evaluation stage in which information is considered and a positive, negative, or neutral evaluation of the product or service is produced. This evaluative judgment is called an attitude. Once this evaluative judgment is made it is often stored to be acted on in the future. Thus, buyers do not have to construct an attitude every time they purchase a product.

Attitudes are among the most frequent measures of consumer response to products and other marketing actions. Most investigators of attitudes would agree that an attitude can be defined as *a learned predisposition to respond in a consistently favorable or unfavorable manner in respect to a given object.*[8] Although an attitude is a predisposition to respond in a particular manner, each attitude includes multiple components:

- *Cognitions* (beliefs). Cognitions or beliefs refer to the total universe of what one thinks or believes to be true about a psychological object. A psychological object may be an idea, event, person, activity, object, product, or company.
- *Affect* (feelings). Affect refers to the nature of the feelings that one holds toward a psychological object. Insofar as attitudes are concerned, feelings may be positive or negative; they cannot be neutral. If one is neutral toward a psychological object, no attitude exists.
- *Intentions.* The term or category, "intentions," refers to behavioral intentions. Intentions are not the behavior itself, but a subjective resolution to behave in a certain way.
- *Overt behavior.* This term refers to public, observable behavior.

Attitudes are formed on the basis of reaction to multiple attributes of an object. Recognition of this fact has led to the development of a whole class of models that have come to be known as *multi-attribute models* of attitude. There are a number of different multi-attribute models, but they all share the common view than an attitude object (a product, store, person, etc.) possesses many attributes (characteristics) that provide the basis for the formation of a consumer's attitude. Multi-attribute models differ from one another primarily in terms of how they view the process by which the individual attributes are put together to form the overall attitude and how they measure various aspects of the model.

Point to Ponder

What cognitions and affects do you have surrounding the ideas that the following words represent? How might this shape your intentions and overt behavior in relation to these words/people/places/brands?

- Subaru
- Disney World
- iPhone
- McDonald's
- President Obama
- President Trump
- The Oscars
- Skydiving

One multi-attribute model that has found widespread use in marketing is the The *Fishbein Model*.[9] The Fishbein model explicitly recognizes that the attitude object may have a number of attributes; this is why this class of models is called multi-attribute. Attitude objects may differ from one another in terms of the degree to which consumers believe that particular attributes are associated with each attribute. In addition, consumers may differ with respect to the value (positive or negative) they assign to each attribute. The Fishbein model makes a clear distinction between intentions and overt behavior; and it does not assume that an individual's overt behavior can be predicted from his or her attitudes. Instead, overt behavior is determined by the individual's intentions.

In the above point to ponder, for example, a consumer may have a strong attitude toward the automobile brand Subaru, but still may not feel that they are in the market for a new car any time soon. Thus, the consumer has no intention of buying one. The overt behavior, in this case, not making a purchase, will follow suit regardless of beliefs and feelings about the brand.

Within the framework of the Fishbein model, the study of attitudes involves three steps: (a) the determination of attitudes; (b) the determination of relevant intentions; and (c) the prediction of overt behavior from intentions. An advantage of this approach is that it systematically examines each stage in the progression from attitudes to intention to overt behavior. And, at each step, it identifies relevant variables. For example, an attitude toward a particular brand would be determined by the following equation, which in simplified form, states:

$$A_b = \sum_{i=1}^{N} W_i B_{ib}$$

where

A_b = the attitude toward a particular brand (the overall evaluation of the brand)

W_i = the weight of importance of attribute i

B_{ib} = the evaluative aspect of belief toward attribute i for brand b

N = the number of attributes important in the selection of a given brand in the given product category.

Within the Fishbein model, this expression defines only the relationship between beliefs (attributes of an object) and attitude; it says nothing about intentions or overt behavior. The relationship between attitudes and intentions must be determined empirically, since two people with the same general attitude may have quite different intentions toward an attitude object. For example, two persons may have the same attitude toward religion, but they may hold different intentions concerning religious behavior. One person might intend to attend church regularly and to pray before meals, but not to donate money to the church or to sing in the church choir. The other person might intend to attend church regularly and donate money to his church, but not to pray before meals or to sing in the church choir.[10]

In addition, individuals may differ with respect to their intentions and with respect to situational constraints that may influence their ability to act on their intentions. For example, two consumers may share very positive attitudes toward Aston Martin automobiles, but one may intend to act on this attitude by purchasing this brand of automobile. On the other hand, the second consumer may have a positive attitude but have no intention of acting on this attitude because he does not have the funds required to purchase such an expensive automobile.

The central role of beliefs in the Fishbein theory suggests that attitude change is best affected by operating on the beliefs of an individual. There are actually four ways to do this:

(a) change the belief itself
(b) change the importance or relative contribution of the belief to the attitude
(c) add a new belief to the attitudinal structure, which changes the weights of the other beliefs as well
(d) change the behavior, that is suggest an alternative behavior that is consistent with the attitude

Takeaways

Human beings may be impacted by numerous outside forces, but they are very active participants in how they process and respond to these forces and evaluate a buying opportunity.

They process through:

- Emotion
- Perception
- Learning
- Memory
- Attitudes

The emotions and motivations for buying are inextricably linked. A person may have this or that force influencing a decision, but emotions are the energy behind buying decisions. Buyer goals whether met, unmet or sought through the buying of a product, evoke emotions. The savvy marketer can energize buyers by triggering these emotions.

As the saying goes, "perception is reality." A consumer's perception of the problem the product seeks to solve and how well that product solves that problem, or meets their goal, drives decision-making. Marketers work to impact consumer perceptions through branding, impactful visuals, advertising, and so on. An important piece of this is how people categorize a brand and distinguish it from its competitors within similar categories.

Marketers do not change perceptions and in turn behavior without recognizing the role of learning. Much of marketing isn't intended to cause an immediate buy decision but rather to build interest, knowledge, and trust in the brand over time. Memory plays a peculiar role in the buying decision because the human brain does not retain everything it encounters. Rather, it chooses to keep certain information and discard the rest. Because of this, marketers use repetition and triggers to aid memorization and learning in much the same way a pre-school teacher may use songs and game to help children remember and internalize colors and their ABCs. All consumers do not memorize and categorize information in the same ways. If a consumer is aspirin-sensitive, then Bayer aspirin may not even be considered a direct competitor of Tylenol. If the consumer simply sees these as painkillers, they do compete. A smart marketer will be aware of how their product is categorized by target consumers.

Consumers and buyers alike may have preconceived notions about a brand that impact how they perceive an ad campaign. These include cognitions, affects, intentions, and overt behavior. As marketers, we must be careful not to misinterpret positive cognition and intention as leading to intentions and overt behavior. It is our job. Fishbein's theory laid out a framework for doing this. Thus far, we have discussed several factors that influence consumer behavior. Next, we will discuss the actually decision-making process.

Notes

1. Reeve (2004).
2. Buck (1988).
3. Holbrook and Hirschman (1982, pp. 132–40).
4. Ormrod (2015).
5. Bettman and Park (1980, pp. 234–48).
6. Sternberg (2006).
7. Stewart (1989, pp. 54–60).
8. Fishbein and Ajzen (1975, p. 6); Ajzen (2005).
9. Fishbein and Ajzen (1975, p. 6); Ajzen (2005).
10. Fishbein and Ajzen (1975, p. 291).

CHAPTER 4

Consumer Behavior as a Decision Process

Chapter 3 introduced a variety of psychological processes that influence how consumers obtain and use information when making purchases. This chapter takes a closer look at specific rubrics and rules that consumers use for making decisions about which products and service to purchase. An understanding of these rubrics and rules is critical for a marketer who wishes to influence consumer's decisions.

A charitable giver, who we will call Samantha, has resolved to give more to help others this year but she does not want to see her money go to waste; she wants to give where she can do the most good. With this goal established, she considers the causes that are most important to her. She then searches for non-profits that support these causes.

She finds the selection overwhelming, so she looks for charities that she has heard of before. She then evaluates them further to narrow down her list, looking at specifically what they do and how they do it, how much of her donor dollar actually goes to help the cause, what others are saying about the charity on the Internet, and how quick and easy it is to donate. She makes her selection. Samantha has just made a buy-decision. The availability of the information she was looking for, as provided by those promoting each organization, influenced where she will contribute her charitable giving.

Ultimately, consumer behavior involves decisions. Thus far we have discussed factors and processes that influence decision-making, but we have not yet discussed the process of decision making. The decision process has at least five steps:

(a) The recognition of a desired goal requiring a decision
(b) Search for alternative ways of satisfying the goal's requirements
(c) An evaluation of the possible alternative solutions
(d) The decision itself
(e) An evaluation of the adequacy of the decision

Consumer decision making in the pursuit of goals is a very complex phenomenon. There are many forms of decision-making. In some cases, the decision-making process is long and difficult. In other cases, decisions are made with so little effort that they are almost automatic and can hardly be called decisions at all. The nature of the consumer's decision-making process is a very important piece of information since it suggests how, and if, the outcome of the process can be modified or reinforced by the marketer.

Types of Consumer Decisions

Consumers do not have unlimited resources for acquiring goods and services. Thus, the problem for the consumer is to find that combination of goods and services that will maximize total utility, given budget and time constraints. The most global of decisions confronting consumers, then, is how they will allocate their budgets and time to the acquisition and consumption of goods and services. Recognition of this most global set of decisions suggests a broad view of competition in the marketplace. It suggests that all goods and services compete for the limited resources of the consumer; competition is not something that occurs only between similar brands.

Allocation Decisions

The first decisions consumers must make are related to the particular goals or desires they wish to satisfy. Does the consumer buy a new car, vacation in Europe, or increase savings? These are quite unrelated products. Yet, for most consumers this type of decision is very real. The question is one of whether the psychic benefits of a European vacation are greater than those of a new car or whether the additional feeling of security associated with a larger savings balance outweighs the psychic benefits of both a vacation and a new car.

Marketers often find themselves confronting the need to help potential customers establish priorities among very different alternatives. Why should a consumer prefer a new car to a vacation in an exotic place? Why should a family forgo a new stereo system to purchase more life insurance? Marketers must be prepared to help consumers set priorities while recognizing that they have rather little control over basic allocation decisions. Allocation decisions are often governed by deep-seated value systems learned over many years from parents, friends, and the society at large. They are not easily influenced, but they are powerful determinants of behavior.

All businesses need to be concerned about allocation decisions, at least at some level. However, for some businesses the allocation decision may be the most important for marketers to influence. For example, a bank or investment firm may need to convince consumers that it is their best interest to spend less and save more. A wellness clinic may suggest that more time should be allocated to exercise rather than other, more sedentary activities. Some firms assist consumers with allocation decisions by offering financing, thereby providing the means for acquiring a product sooner rather than later.

Product Category Decisions

When the consumer has established basic priorities for resource allocation at a given point in time, other decisions follow. Having decided to save funds for the future, does the consumer invest in stocks and bonds, place money in a savings account in a local bank, or buy life insurance with investment value? These alternatives may all accomplish the same end but differ in the means by which the end is accomplished and the level of risk the consumer must bear. The decision to be made among these alternatives is one of product category.

Point to Ponder

What types of businesses focus their marketing activities on the product category decisions? How do these types of businesses market their products and services?

Product Form Decisions

Once a particular product category has been selected, the consumer may still be faced with the choice of product type or form. Lawnmowers can be of the push mower, self-propelled, or riding variety. Deodorant comes in cream, stick, aerosol, and roll-on forms. Automobiles come in a variety of styles, makes, and types.

Brand Decisions

Finally, a choice of brand must be made. Sometimes this is the last of the decisions to be made, sometimes the brand is selected first, then the particular product form or type. For example, there is evidence to suggest that consumers select a brand of deodorant first, then select the particular type. For other categories, the product form decision is made first.

More Decisions

All of the foregoing decisions are product-related. There are, however, still other decisions the consumer must face. One is the timing of the purchase. Should the new car be bought at the beginning, middle, or end of the model year? Should a purchase be made immediately, or delayed in hopes of a lower price or the availability of a higher performance product at a later date?

The consumer must also select an outlet for the acquisition of a product or service. Brick and mortar stores, online websites, catalogs, and direct response advertising are all options for purchasing many products. Even among bricks and mortar stores, some retailers are more expensive than others but may offer significant service during and after the sale. Some outlets may offer a wide assortment of products and accessories, while others offer only the basic product without frills or accessories. When selecting an outlet or vendor the consumer may have to decide whether a higher price is worth the additional service provided, or whether a lower price is worth dispensing with the convenience and reliability of the service offerings.

While the product and outlet decision may be independent, they frequently are not. Since not all outlets or dealers carry all products or brands, the two decisions influence one another. The selection of a particular outlet may preclude consideration of some products, and vice versa. In fact, when the consumer makes a retailer selection before making a product decision it becomes very important for the marketer to have very extensive distribution by being represented in as many outlets as possible. On the other hand, if the consumer makes the product decision prior to the retail outlet decision the marketer can use a more selective distribution strategy because it is likely that the consumer will seek out a retailer that carries his or her desired product. This is but one example of how a seemingly simple decision, or in this case, a sequence of decisions, by the buyer has profound implications for marketing strategy.

The Nature of Consumer and Buyer Decision Making

The decision process can be viewed as a problem-solving situation in which the problem is defined as the need to achieve a particular goal, a need to move from an existing state of affairs and a desired state of affairs. Within this view, products are goal enablers or solutions to problems.

Stages in the Problem-Solving Process

In a classic work that continues to influence research on problem solving today, John Dewey defined five stages in problem solving.[1] His definitions have been widely accepted as the standard or classic paradigm for problem-solving activity and, with minor modifications, are well adapted to describing consumer behavior. Dewey's five stages, adapted to consumer behavior, are shown in Figure 4.1.

The amount of activity associated with each stage may vary greatly, depending on the product being purchased and the circumstances surrounding its acquisition. For example, we normally spend more time at each stage in buying a new automobile than in buying a box of laundry detergent. Also, a product we purchase for the first time will normally require more consideration than a purchase for which we have had previous experience.

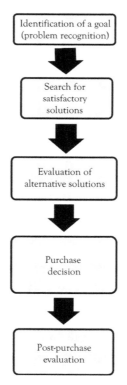

Figure 4.1 Stages in consumer decision-making

Each stage of the problem-solving process has somewhat different implications for marketing in that certain marketing activities are more appropriate at some stages than at others. It should also be recognized, of course, that different consumers are in different stages of the decision process at different times, so that a balanced marketing program requires a variety of activities, each designed to facilitate purchase at one or more stages of the decision process.

Point to Ponder

How can marketers influence and shape the various stages of decision making? Can marketers influence buyer's perceptions of how important and urgent a problem is? How?

Search for Satisfactory Solutions

A critical stage in consumer decision-making is the search of information and a satisfactory solution, that is, shopping. Normally, the search for a satisfactory solution takes the form of gathering information, casually or systematically, about alternative products and/or brands. The search process may be virtually instantaneous—as, for example, in impulse decisions or in emergencies—or it may involve intensive exploration over a prolonged period of time—as would normally be the case in the purchase of a house, a car, or some other major item.

Point to Ponder

Some marketing professionals talk about "external memory." By this they mean things in the store or other shopping environments that facilitate recall and retrieval of information or that relieves the shopper from remembering detailed information, such as a specific price point or performance information. In what situations might such external memory aids be most useful for a marketer? Are there situations in which relying on such memory aids could disadvantage a firm?

Bettman has suggested a distinction between two types of product information search: internal search, the search for product information stored in memory; and external search, the active acquisition of product information through shopping, talking to others, and other sources of information.[2] There is some evidence that these two types of search are substitutes, one serving in the place of the other.

Evaluation of Alternative Solutions

Even when alternatives are retrieved from memory it may be necessary to update information and locate the alternative. This is what shopping, or external search, is about. A substantial literature has been developed on the amount and determinants of external search among consumers. One striking conclusion emerges from this literature: most consumers engage in very limited external information search, even for high ticket items.

For example, several studies have shown that a significant number of purchasers (often a third or more) of automobiles and major appliances consider no more than a single make or brand prior to purchase and visit only one dealer.[3] For less expensive items the amount of information search tends to be even less. These findings suggest that systematic information gathering prior to many purchases is quite limited. This does not mean that buyers are irrational. Rather, it means that in many cases they rely on memory and in other cases the value of obtaining information is not worth the time and effort.

Shopping can take a variety of forms. It may involve visits to retail outlets, perusal of advertising and manufacturer's brochures, search on the Internet, product reviews, discussions with friends or sales personnel, reading books and magazines about the product category, consultation of consumer magazines such as *Consumer Reports*, and actual product trial. While the amount of search may be small for most consumers, there is substantial variation in both the amount and pattern of search activities across buyers. Studies reveal that 10–20 percent of shoppers engage in extensive information search.[4] In between the non-searchers and heavy searchers is a wide range of more modest searchers.

Shopping is influenced by a complex array of factors. Some studies have found greater product experience leads to less external search, but others have found no relationship, and still others have found that moderate amounts of previous product experience lead to the greatest information search. These contradictory findings are best explained by recognizing that prior product experience interacts with a wide range of other factors to determine the amount of external search. For example, if the previous experience has been satisfactory, it is likely to result in lesser search, but if the prior experience is unsatisfactory, external search may be great. A consumer who knows little about a product may do little search on the first purchase occasion, perhaps relying on a friend's recommendation, then do more search as he becomes more familiar with the product category and the features he should be evaluating.

A number of situational factors affect external research. These factors include: urgency;[5] the number and proximity of retail outlets;[6] the existence of substantive price differences among product alternatives when the absolute price of products in the category is high;[7] and the amount of enjoyment derived from the shopping experience itself.[8]

Consumers also have preferences for certain types of information and information sources in particular purchase situations. Few consumers appear to rely on a single source of product information, although there may be a preferred source at a given point in the purchase process. For example, mass media appears to be used more during the early stages of the purchase process when consumers are trying to identify potential alternatives.[9] Interpersonal sources of information appear to be more frequently used nearer the actual purchase decision, particularly for high involvement products. Different media also appear to be used to obtain different types of information. When the physical appearance of a product, including its styling and design, are important to the consumer, television appears to be a primary source of information.[10]

On the other hand, it is difficult to provide styling information about some products in a television medium. The styling of furniture and carpets are often better illustrated in print because consumers apparently need to see these products in living, static color to think about them and to visualize them in their homes. Most people are aware the computer screens and televisions can distort color. In addition, complex, socially visible products are more likely to evoke information search among interpersonal sources, perceived experts, opinion leaders, and friends.[11]

Making Decisions

Consumers evaluate information as they gather it, accepting, discounting, or discarding information as it appears relevant and/or trustworthy. In recent years marketers have become interested in the specific decision rules that consumers use when selecting a product. These rules involve the attributes actually considered when making a purchase, sometimes called the *determinant attributes*, the relative weight given these attributes, and the way in which product information is put together to arrive at a decision.

Frequently, consumers use simple rules of thumb, or heuristics, to reduce the effort involved in making product decisions. Such heuristics abound in the marketplace: "buy the cheapest"; "buy whatever is on sale"; "always buy from vendor X"; "always buy brand Y"; "buy person Z's recommended brand"; "buy the product that comes to mind first"; and "buy the most expensive, since price means quality." There is no end to the number of heuristics consumers may use in making decisions. A consumer who cannot evaluate the refrigeration unit of a refrigerator may use the sturdiness of shelves and the quality of paint on the refrigerator to evaluate overall quality. Another consumer, unable to evaluate all of the mechanical attributes of an automobile, may use the quality of the stitching in the upholstery as an indicator of quality.

Even when consumers are knowledgeable about a product category and could consider numerous attributes, they may use heuristics to reduce the effort involved in information search and in thinking about the decision.[12] Thus, a consumer may always buy a particular brand or purchase from a particular vendor because he or she has always been satisfied with that product or vendor in the past. Alternatively, a consumer may have learned from prior experience that products really differ on only one or two attributes. Those may be the only attributes considered in the purchase process even after new products have expanded the number of product attribute differences in the category. Recognition that consumers frequently employ heuristics for decision-making has led marketers to examine heuristic decision making and the situations in which it will occur rather than more systematic decision-making.[13]

Consumers confront an enormous number of decisions as they pursue their goals and seek solutions to problems. In order to simplify decision-making consumers frequently employ decision-making strategies and decision-making rules that help them reduce the time and effort required. For many purchase occasions consumers "program" decisions. A programmed decision generally has three characteristics:

(a) It involves a repetitive act
(b) It is satisfied by a routine procedure
(c) It requires no special thought on the part of the purchaser.[14]

These types of decisions are essentially "habit." Much of buyer's behavior is based on programmed decisions because such decisions are both efficient and satisfying. Brand loyalty is a special case of a programmed decision where the purchase of a specific brand has become habitual.

Takeaways

The decision process has at least five steps:

(a) The recognition of a desired goal requiring a decision
(b) A search for alternative ways of satisfying the goal's requirements
(c) An evaluation of the possible alternative solutions
(d) The decision itself
(e) An evaluation of the adequacy of the decision

Consumer choices are not infinite. They have budget and time constraints. On the larger scale, all products and services no matter how unrelated are competing for these limited resources. This may require you to help consumers establish priorities. Many of these priorities are deep-seated and difficult to change. With others you may have more influence.

Once a person has moved beyond choosing a category into which they will spend their limited time and money, they must make product form decisions like gas versus electric mower. Only after they have moved past the first two stages, do they begin to consider a brand. As a marketer, you must be there guiding the buyer through each level of the buying decision.

When to buy and where to buy will also play their role. A marketer helps influence the when by creating a sense of urgency through special offers, fear of missing out, establishing timing priorities, and so on. Where a person buys may be the result of other products or services that the person plans to buy at the same time, leading you to plan your branding and distribution strategies around the bigger picture.

Dewey's theory suggests that there five stages of problem-solving that impact decision-making to varying degrees. Consumers and buyers alike first identify their goals. They then begin to search for satisfactory solutions. During this phase, they will recall stored information. This is where those repetitive advertisements, brand awareness efforts and providing of information to people before they are even considering buying come back to the surface to influence decisions. Active information-gathering will ensue. The consumer will then evaluate various alternatives. Some mediums have shown themselves more effective than others during this evaluation process.

The consumer will then compile all of the information, discarding any that seems less relevant or trustworthy, in order to make a buy-decision. This does not, however, end the decision-making process as the consumer must receive the product or service and then evaluate how well in met the goals established at the beginning of the process. This stage may lead to returns, reviews (good or bad), referrals, re-buying, or simply making a different choice next time.

The next chapter will focus more closely look the decision-making process by exploring programmed decisions and decision-making rules.

Notes

1. Dewey (1910).
2. Bettman (1979).
3. Furse, Punj, and Stewart (1984, pp. 417–31).
4. Claxton, Fry, and Portis (1974, pp. 35–42).
5. Ibid.
6. Cort and Dominguez (1977, pp. 187–92); Nelson (1974, pp. 311–29).
7. Newman and Staelin (1972, pp. 249–57).
8. Katona and Mueller (1955, pp. 30–87).
9. Berning, Kohn, and Jacoby (1974, pp. 18–22).
10. Houston (1979, pp. 135–44).

11. Claxton, Fry, and Portis (1974, pp. 35–42).
12. Shugan (1980, pp. 99–111).
13. Eagly and Chaiken (1993).
14. Runyon and Stewart (1987).

CHAPTER 5

Mapping the Market: Decision Making Rules

The translation of consumer's behavior and decision-making into marketing strategies and actions can be aided through the development of product or service "maps" that provide a picture of what consumers desire and what competitive alternatives offer. This chapter describes market maps, how such maps are constructed, and how such maps inform marketing strategy.

Terrence has grocery shopping down to a science. With a list in hand and the store mapped out in his head, he walks up and down each aisle in the same pattern each visit. He starts in the produce section and works his way through the store, skipping only the cookie and baking aisles because he has nothing on this list in those locations. Pulling items from the shelves one after the other, he barely loses stride. It takes him less than a second to decide which product to buy because he has already bought each item more than a thousand times. There is no question which brand he will choose, size, or flavor. He knows what the package looks like and goes right for it.

Within an hour, Terrence is in the checkout line. He is not even tempted by the impulse buys in the checkout. He has already decided that he will never buy anything while waiting in line. Terrence never overspends because he knows exactly what he will get going in and only gets items on the list.

Terrence does not know that he has grocery shopping down to a science. His behavior has simply developed over time as part of the brain's natural, habit-forming process. As he continued to shop for the same items over and over, his brand choices and shopping habits became programmed. Items are always in the same place, so he never has to look for anything. For him, grocery shopping has become a mindless co-pilot driven act. Now, consider what Terrence would do if something were to disrupt his routine.

What would happen if his partner put a new item on the shopping list? What would Terrence do if he found that his favorite brand was out-of-stock? Suppose Terrence encounters a friend in the checkout who points out a story in a news magazine that the friend thought was particularly interesting? Each circumstance may disrupt Terrence's well-practiced shopping routine and he will need to reprogram his approach to shopping. Marketers are often interested in getting consumers to reprogram their shopping routines—to check out their products instead of the one the consumer always buys?

Alert marketers recognize the importance of reaching consumers before their brand decisions become routinized or programmed. This is why so much advertising and promotion is directed toward young markets through "teen," "bridal," and special youth media. Although programmed decisions may take a number of forms, one particularly important type of programmed decision is brand loyalty. A buyer who has "programmed" a decision based on brand is very valuable to a firm and very difficult for competitors to change.

Other decisions are not programmed. Non-programmed decisions generally occur when the shopping situation exhibits one or more of the following characteristics:[1]

(a) the purchase or purchasing situation new or novel in some respect;

(b) the purchase is psychologically, socially or financially important;

(c) the purchase is complex; and/or

(d) the purchase does not lend itself to routine solutions.

Point to Ponder

Brand loyalty could be construed as either the use of a heuristic, a programmed decision, or both. What might this suggest about the value of a brand? What might this suggest about marketing strategies for overcoming loyalty to a competitor's brand?

The purchase of an automobile, a large appliance, a major item of clothing, expensive jewelry, household furnishings, wedding presents, or any number of other purchase decisions made by consumers may be of a non-programmed nature, though these too can become programmed. There is no set pattern for handling a non-programmed decision because each case has unique features that consumers have not encountered before or have encountered so infrequently that their past experience is of little value. In such situations, consumers are "open" to information and often diligently seek it out. Their search for a satisfactory solution may be extended, involving a great deal of time and effort, or it may be limited. In either case, consumers will give it no more time and effort than they think it is worth.

High and Low Involvement Purchase Decisions

It is frequently useful to make distinctions between high and low involvement purchases by buyers. Such distinctions are useful because there is ample evidence that consumers behave differently according to whether the situation is one of high or low involvement.[2] A low-involvement decision may be a more likely candidate to become a programmed decision.

There is much debate about what involvement actually means and how it should be measured. What may be a high involvement situation for one consumer may be low involvement for another. Generally, high involvement is characterized by a high degree of personal goal relevance and some personal identification with the outcome of a purchase decision. It is a reflection of the perceived importance of the purchase. The higher the level of involvement in a purchase situation, the more motivated the consumer will be to obtain information and process that information in a more thorough and systematic fashion. In low involvement situations the buyer may not view the cost of such systematic information search and processing to be worth the effort. In these situations, the buyer is more likely to rely on simple rules of thumb, heuristics, to make a decision.

Thus, consumer decision-making processes may take two forms, effortful, systematic processing or near effortless heuristic processing. Either of these two processes may, in turn, be programmed, that is automatic, or non-programmed, that is involving some effort to construct a decision-making strategy. Yet, these forms of decision-making represent extremes on a continuum. There are a variety of decision strategies that consumers may employ, and these strategies vary considerably in the effort they require. It is important for the marketer to understand these rules, whether they are more systematic or more heuristic in nature, because the decision-making strategy used by the consumer often determines the outcome of the purchase process. A key element of decision making strategies is formal decision rules. Understanding the rules consumers use when making a purchase decision is especially useful to marketers because such an understanding provides what in analogous to a map of the market, that is, it provides information about the route the customer takes to get to the purchase decision.

Decision Rules

Decision rules may be divided into two broad classes—compensatory rules and non-compensatory rules. Compensatory rules involve the simultaneous consideration of alternatives on a number of attributes. Non-compensatory rules involve consideration of alternatives one or a few attributes at a time. A heuristic is an extreme form of a non-compensatory model since it involves consideration of only one attribute. We will discuss compensatory rules first, then turn our attention to several common non-compensatory rules.

Compensatory Rules

The linear compensatory rule involves the simultaneous consideration of multiple attributes for each alternative. Each attribute may be weighted differently, or all attributes may have the same weight. This rule allows the consumer to consider a variety of attributes and make trade-offs among them. Thus, an alternative that is poor on one attribute may still be considered acceptable because it is high on other attributes. A deficiency on one attribute may be compensated for by another attribute. The Fishbein model of attitudes discussed earlier in Chapter 3 is an example of a compensatory rule.

Compensatory rules require a substantial amount of information processing and assume that the consumer is attempting to make an optimal or "best" decision. The frequency of use of this rule varies from product to product. One study found that approximately one third of car buyers used some type of compensatory rule.[3] Because this decision strategy involves considerable effort, it is less frequently used in purchase situations that involve little cost or risk, that is, in situations involving low involvement purchases.

When consumers use a compensatory rule, it is important for the marketer to know which attributes are employed and the relative weights assigned each attribute. Since it is the overall evaluation of the product that is important, the marketer has greater latitude in product design. Some features, such as lower price, might be used to offset other characteristics of the product. Table 5.1 provides an illustration how a compensatory decision rule might operate in practice.

Point to Ponder

In what types of situations are buyers most likely to use a compensatory rule? Do the methods of attitude change discussed earlier suggest any strategies that might be useful for influencing compensatory decision-making rules?

Table 5.1 Example of a compensatory decision rule

Consider the buyer of a new car. This buyer considers four attributes of cars to be important and weights them as follow:

Attribute	Weight	The buyer has also identified three possible alternatives for purchase that all cost about the same. The buyer perceives the cars to perform on the four attributes as follows:
Gas Mileage	.2	
Dependability	.4	
Styling	.3	Performance (1-10 scale)
Road Handling	.1	

Attribute	Model 1	Model 2	Model 3
Gas Mileage	8	9	5
Dependability	4	5	5
Styling	9	5	8
Road Handling	4	5	10

Applying a compensatory decision rule produced the following overall evaluation of each model:

Evaluation of Car 1 = .2(8) + .4(4) + .3(9) + .1(4) = 6.3

Evaluation of Car 2 = .2(9) + .4(5) + .3(5) + .1(5) = 5.8

Evaluation of Car 3 = .2(5) + .4(5) + .3(8) + .1(10) = $\boxed{6.4}$ "Best" Alternative

Point to Ponder

This outcome illustrates an important feature of compensatory models: a poor showing on one characteristic can be compensated for by a good showing on other attributes. Thus, Car No. 3 receives the highest overall evaluation despite being considerably below the other alternatives with respect to gas mileage. The evaluations of the other attributes made up for the poor showing on gas mileage. Why was price not considered in the evaluations? If there were differences in price, how would these influence the outcome of the decision?

Noncompensatory Rules

Other decision rules, sometimes called noncompensatory rules, do not provide for the types of trade-offs that are involved in compensatory rules. Noncompensatory rules may take a variety of forms and may be highly idiosyncratic. These rules are not fictions; they are selected by the buyer to serve whatever purpose he or she has in mind. In fact, use of these types of rules is far more common than use of compensatory rules. Some of the more common noncompensatory rules are summarized in Table 5.2.

Table 5.2 Types of noncompensatory decision rules

(1) The *conjunctive rule* assumes that the consumer has established a minimum acceptable standard on each product attribute. This decision strategy requires consideration of all attributes of product alternatives but is noncompensatory. Any product that does not meet the minimum acceptable standard on any attribute is eliminated from further consideration, no matter how well it does on other attributes. The conjunctive rule requires less effort than compensatory rules because it can be applied to one brand at a time. All brands do not have to be considered simultaneously; rather, each brand may be compared to the standard. Several brands may meet the acceptable standard on all attributes, however. This may mean that some other decision rule must be employed to make a final selection. The conjunctive rule is commonly used as a screening tool to reduce the number of brands given further consideration.

(2) The *disjunctive rule* also requires that buyers establish a minimum level of performance for each product attribute. Typically, this level of performance is set high when using the disjunctive rule. Brands that meet the minimum standard on at least one attribute are given further consideration. This rule seldom yields a single alternative, which means that the disjunctive rule is most often used as a screening strategy followed by application of another decision rule. For example, in selecting a restaurant, a consumer may select those alternatives that are within 15 minutes drive, or provide quick service, or allow a customer to call in an order before arriving. Any restaurant meeting any one of these criteria would be considered acceptable.

(3) The *lexicographic rule* is the most common decision strategy employed by consumers. It is a very simple strategy that requires that consumers evaluate alternatives on only one attribute at a time. The lexicographic rule requires that consumers rank attributes in the order of their importance. Consumers select the brand, or brands, that perform best on the most important attribute. Only those brands that tie on the most important attribute are given further consideration. Brands that tie on the second most important attribute are evaluated on the third most important attribute. This process of single attribute comparison continues until only a single alternative is left.

(4) The *affect referral rule* does not involve consideration of product attributes. Rather, it involves the recollection of an overall evaluation of each alternative. This overall evaluation may grow out of the consumer's prior experiences with products or from a strong positive feeling obtained from advertising, a sales representative, or other source. The evaluation is quite holistic, which makes it very resistant to change as long as the consumer continues to have positive experiences with the product selected.

In many cases buyers use a *combination of rules*. As noted, some decision rules are more likely to result in a single alternative than others. Some rules appear better suited for narrowing the number of alternatives for further consideration. Compensatory rules are effortful and practically impossible with large numbers of brands. As a result, decision rules may be applied in combination or in sequence.

Post-purchase Evaluation

The decision process does not stop with the actual purchase of a brand. Post-purchase evaluation is a critical step in the process because it serves as an important influence on future behavior. The consumer who is disappointed in product performance is not likely to repurchase, nor to recommend it to others, if there is an acceptable alternative available. The dissatisfied consumer may complain and seek redress. The satisfied customer may, on the other hand, spread word of the product to friends and neighbors, buy more of the product, buy more often, or provide opportunities for others to try the product. The purchase process seldom ends with a single purchase. Rather, the consumer makes an evaluation of whether a product has solved the problem for which it was intended.

While consumer satisfaction may, on the surface, appear to be a simple phenomenon, it is really quite complex, since the degree of satisfaction may be related to the level of consumer expectations rather than to absolute product performance. For example, a major food company developed a blueberry muffin mix that, in blind taste tests, was strongly preferred by consumers over major competitive products. The new brand, priced competitively, was convenient to make and obtained wide distribution. A strong advertising effort, featuring "fresh-picked" Michigan blueberries, performed exceedingly well in copy tests. With everything going for him, the product manager had high hopes for a successful test market. In test markets, however, initial trial was high, but product repurchase was low. In follow-up surveys, consumers expressed disappointment in product performance—"It just didn't taste as good as it looked on TV." This occurred despite consumers preferring this product to competition in blind product tests. Thus, disappointment of expectations—not actual product quality—led to the failure to repurchase.

Understanding Customer Satisfaction

The complexity of satisfaction judgment is illustrated by the "two-factor theory of satisfaction."[4] This theory suggests that customers judge products on a limited set of attributes, some of which (determinant attributes) are relatively important in determining satisfaction. Other factors not critical to satisfaction are related to dissatisfaction when performance on them is unsatisfactory.

In the past two decades, a substantial literature has been developed on consumer satisfaction/dissatisfaction (CS/D).[5] This literature suggests that consumer dissatisfaction with products is pervasive, but unlikely to result in much action on the part of the consumer. In one of the largest studies of its kind, Best and Andreasen found that about 20 percent of all purchases produced some dissatisfaction.[6] This same study found that few dissatisfied consumers complain to the seller and only about 40 percent of dissatisfied customers take any action to correct the perceived problem with the product. Individual consumers who do complain appear to be atypical of most consumers. Those who do complain tend to be better educated, have higher incomes, are more politically active and more active in formal organizations, and tend to be more liberal in their political orientation.[7]

While it is clear that satisfaction/dissatisfaction is related to the degree to which a product meets the consumer's expectations, it is less clear how these expectations interact with various characteristics of consumers and products to produce a sense of satisfaction or dissatisfaction. For example, a product can perform in exactly the same way for two different consumers, but one consumer may be satisfied while the other is dissatisfied because they brought different expectations to the product usage situation, have different experiences with alternatives, and different expertise related to product use.

For the marketer, customer satisfaction is critical to insure repeat purchases and positive word-of-mouth about the product. The challenge to insuring such satisfaction is that consumers seldom voice their complaints to the seller or make other efforts to obtain satisfaction. More often they simply buy a competitive product on the next purchase occasion. This means customers may be lost and the marketer never knows why. For this reason, many firms have sought to encourage legitimate product complaints and establish mechanisms for handling consumer problems. Consumer hot lines (toll-free numbers) provide an easy means for consumers to register complaints. Comment cards, found in virtually all hotels and many restaurants, provide another means for obtaining information about consumer's satisfaction/dissatisfaction.

While these approaches are useful, they do not capture the majority of consumers who experience product performance problems. As a result, many firms use proactive methods for identifying product problems. Many firms have established ongoing programs of market research in which representative consumers are sought out and asked about their experiences with products. Such research may go so far as to visit customers in their homes or offices to discuss product satisfaction as the customer actually uses the product.

Point to Ponder

Is every sale a good sale? If a customer is not satisfied with a product would it have been better had the customer not purchased the product in the first instance? Are there circumstances when a firm should discourage a potential customer from buying?

Mapping Markets

One of the most useful tools for integrating information about consumer's perceptions and decision-making are product maps, sometimes called perceptual maps. Product maps are pictures of the structure of a market: product or service offerings are placed in an attribute or benefit space so that the manager can readily see how his or her offerings compare to competitor's offerings. It is also possible to map the preferred level of each attribute or feature on the map for each segment in the market, thereby providing an indication of which segments are attracted to which

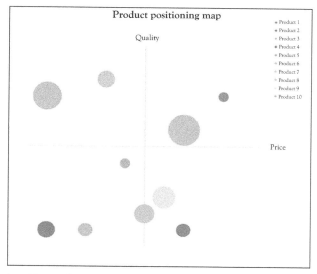

Figure 5.1 Example of product map

offerings and why. Figure 5.1 provides an example of a product map. In this map, there are two segments: segment 1 prefers a high-quality product and will pay a high price for it; segment 2 prefers a lower-priced product and will give up some quality to obtain the lower price. The size of the product symbols represents the size of the sales of each product. Note that the distribution of products suggests that there is considerable diversity in how consumers make trade-offs between price and quality or that there are other characteristics of the products that also influence product preference.

Point to Ponder

Why are there no products in the upper left-hand quadrant of the product map in Figure 5.1?

Requirements for Product Mapping

The creation of a product map requires several types of information about consumers. First, it requires identification of the product or service alternatives from which a customer might select. This may seem like a simple question but is often quite complex. An important competitor might be a "home-made" solution that is not a commercial product in the category under consideration. For example, white distilled vinegar is often used as a household cleaner instead of commercial cleaning products. When such substitutes exist in a market, it is important that they be represented in the product map.

It is also often the case that the most important consumer decision to understand is related to how to spend money or time, rather than selection of a specific alternative from an array of like products. Thus, the marketer for a professional sports team may find it more useful to map noncomparable alternatives for spending leisure time and discretionary income because such alternatives as live theatre, music concerts, and even an afternoon at the beach may be more important competitors than another sporting event.

The easiest way to determine what alternative to include in a map is to ask consumers to identify the alternative they consider for obtaining particular benefits or solving specific problems. It is, however, important to frame the question in terms of how the consumer approaches the world. In the cleaning product example above, a consumer asked about which commercial cleaning products they use might not name vinegar even if they use it for cleaning because they do not identify it as a commercial cleaning product. Similarly, in the sports example, asking consumers about sports events is unlikely to elicit non-sports events that may be important sources of competition.

The second piece of information required to construct a product map is the set of product features or attributes that consumers use for selecting among alternatives. Again, asking consumers can be a simple way to obtain such information. A question such as, "when thinking about your next automobile purchase, what factors will be important in your decision?" is usually sufficient to obtain information about relevant attributes. For any one consumer, there are unlikely to be more than 3–4 really important attributes that influence purchase decisions, but in very diverse markets with numerous segments, there can be attributes that are important to some consumers and not others.

Once the relevant product alternatives and important attributes are identified there is a need to obtain consumer's perceptions of how each alternative stacks-up on each attribute and how important each attribute is to the consumers decision. Such information can generally be obtained using simple survey rating scales, which then provide the input for construction of the product map.

Constructing Product Maps

The actual construction of product maps can range from very simple, intuitive maps based on management judgment to very complex approaches employing sophisticated statistical methods. It is important to recognize that any such construction should have its roots in consumer's perceptions and decision-making. Thus, if management judgment is used is important that the managers providing such judgments be very familiar with customers.

Takeaways

Once a consumer's decision has been programmed, it will likely require considerable time and money to change that programming. For this reason, the alert marker should attend to reaching people before a decision is programmed. Decisions that are new, impactful to the mind or wallet, or complex are more likely to remain unprogrammed because they are high-involvement decisions.

Consumers and buyers use decision strategies to make these unprogrammed decisions. They use compensatory rules, which allow them to evaluate multiple products with varying attributes at once, weighing the pros and cons of each. This strategy requires incredible use of brain power and it, therefore, limited to high-risk decisions by the average consumer. Ultimately, the consumer must decide if advantage A overcomes shortcoming B.

More commonly consumers apply noncompensatory rules. These rules, while still methodical, may vary more greatly among groups. We discussed, for example, the conjunctive rule which allows consumers to immediately eliminate a large number of choices because they don't meet certain pre-established standards for certain attributes. This is noncompensatory because the choice is eliminated regardless of whether another attribute may have somehow compensated for this attribute's shortcoming.

After the purchase is made, and the product or service received, consumers apply similar rules to evaluate how satisfied they are with the result. Their expectations prior to purchase can strongly influence satisfaction more-so than actual quality. Many consumers do not voice their dissatisfaction, leaving it to marketers to generate feedback and read between the lines when there is little to be had.

Mapping markets is a great way to better understand how your target customers make decisions, which allows you to evaluate attributes in a visual way from the standpoint of consumers. The best mapping results not when we make assumptions but from in-depth surveying of consumers regarding their decision-making process. Next, let us take a look specifically at how decisions are made within organizations.

Notes

1. Runyon and Stewart (1987).
2. Zaichkowsky (1985, pp. 341–52).
3. Reilly and Holman (1977, pp. 185–90).
4. Swan and Combs (1976, pp. 25–33).
5. Hill and Alexander (2006); Denove and Power IV (2006).
6. Best and Andreason (1976).
7. Warland, Herman, and Williams (1975, pp. 104–15).

CHAPTER 6

Organizational Buyer Behavior

Purchases are often made for and on behalf of organizations rather the individual consumer. Organizational purchasing involves the same processes that have been described in previous chapters, but there is an added layer of complexity that reflects the dynamics of the organization. This chapter provides an introduction to organizational purchasing behavior.

Maria is the purchasing manager for a small hospital in a major city. She is responsible for ordering, receiving, and inventorying all of the pharmaceutical products used by the hospital. In order to do her job, she carries out the instructions of the formulary committee that is composed of physicians, nurses, and pharmacists who meet to determine what drugs the hospital will purchase and stock. She also must stay abreast of the ever-changing government regulations related to pharmaceutical products and the willingness of insurers to pay for specific products. The CFO of the hospital checks in every week to monitor spending on pharmaceutical products. She spends large portions of her day in meetings with others to discuss purchasing policies. Her day is often interrupted by sales personnel for pharmaceutical companies and physicians lobbying for their favorite product or on behalf of a patient who needs an exception to the approved list of products. Maria is a buyer, but only one of many contributors and influencers in the purchase decision. Such is the nature of purchases by organizations.

Point to Ponder

A common assumption about organizational buyer behavior is that it is more "rational" and objective than individual buyer behavior and that economic criteria are the primary determinants of organizational decision making. Do you agree? What kinds of noneconomic factors may influence organizational buying behavior?

Much of this book has focused on the individual decision maker in purchasing situations. This is appropriate because decision-making is inherently a human enterprise regardless of the ultimate customer for a product. This book would not be complete, however, if it did not address the specific issues that arise when organizations are customers. Organizations have needs (raw materials, operating supplies, etc.), seek information on product alternatives, make choices among those alternatives, evaluate the product in use, and make evaluations of satisfaction.

Many factors influence the purchase decision of an organization. Although it is not often recognized, business-to-business marketing accounts for more than half of all economic activity in the United States. In the international arena, most market transactions are between organizations. Of course, many of these transactions involve products and services that are eventually sold to end-user consumers, there is often an intermediate sale from one organization, say a manufacturer, to another organization, such as a distributor.

Despite the fact that the size of many organizational purchases dwarfs those of individual consumers, organizational consumers have been less frequently studied. One reason for this is that organizational buying behavior tends to be more complex than the buying behavior of individual consumers. Organizational buying frequently involves many individuals.

Social and individual differences play a different role in organizational purchasing than in the purchase behavior of individual consumers. The characteristics of each of these individuals, as well as the interactions among them, influence the purchase process and consumption of goods and services, but play a lesser role in defining needs. Political factors also play a greater role in the decision-making of organizations than in the purchase behavior of individual consumers.

Differences Between Individual and Organizational Buying Behavior

Table 6.1 provides a summary of some of the key differences between individual consumer behavior and organizational buying behavior. However, these differences do not begin to capture the complexity associated with organizational buying. Relationships among organizations can become quite complex. The same organization can simultaneously be a customer, competitor, and supplier for another organization. For example, IBM competes with Intel in the manufacture of computer chips but also purchases computer chips from Intel. At the same time, IBM has been a major supplier of Intel, even winning Intel's Preferred Supplier Quality Award. Such complexity obviously requires management, and such relationships are very common. They are found in financial services,

Table 6.1 Differences between consumer purchasing and organizational purchasing

Consumer Purchasing	Organizational Purchasing
Primary Demand	Derived Demand
Lesser Focus on Economic Objectives	Greater Focus on Economic Objectives
Many Customers	Fewer Customers
Smaller Purchase Volumes	Smaller Purchase Volumes
Less Sophisticated Buyers	Sophisticated, Professional Buyers
Less Complex Buying Process	More Complex Buying Process with More Influences
Less Power Relative to Marketer	Greater Power Relative to Marketers
Greater Influence of Advertising	Greater Influence of Personal Selling
Greater Indirect Distribution	Greater Direct Distribution

in the computer and electronics industry, in the aerospace industry, and a whole range of other types of businesses.

The Organizational Purchase Process

Like individual and household purchase decisions, organizational purchases take a variety of forms ranging from simple to complex. Different types of purchases result in different processes, so it is more appropriate to discuss purchase processes rather than a single process. Three different types of organizational purchase processes have been identified:[1]

(a) The straight rebuy, which is a routine and recurring purchase. It typically requires little information search and vendors are usually selected from a pre-specified list;

(b) The modified rebuy, which is also a recurring purchase, but with changes in either the product specifications or acceptable vendors;

(c) The new task, which is a purchase situation that has not occurred before. New tasks establish patterns for future rebuys and require extensive information acquisition.

Each of these purchase types makes different demands on the organization and offers different challenges to the marketer. The straight rebuy is a simple process often performed by clerical personnel. When stock runs low, a new order may automatically be triggered. This situation is comfortable for the marketer who is on the approved list of vendors but represents a difficult problem for the vendor who is not. The unapproved vendor must get the buyer to redefine the task. Typically, most organizations resist changing a routine purchase to something involving more effort. Only real benefits, superior performance, lower costs, higher quality, or faster delivery, are likely to justify a change in vendors.

In general, when organizations confront a new buying task, as defined by the newness of the purchase and the need for product information, the purchase task will be characterized by a large number of persons involved in the decision process; a long time before a decision is made; uncertainty about needs and the relative appropriateness of alternative solutions; greater concern for finding a good solution rather than a low price or assured supply; greater influence by technical personnel and less influence by purchasing agents; and a greater willingness to entertain proposals from a larger array of potential suppliers including new suppliers.[2]

An understanding of the type of task facing an organization has important implications for marketing organizations in terms of both efficient allocation of resources and the design of marketing strategies. A small and unknown supplier will have great difficulty getting a hearing from a potential customer in the rebuy stage, even when it has a superior product. New tasks offer the best opportunities for creating a buyer–seller relationship.

Stages in the New Buy Purchase Process

Like purchases by individual consumers, the organizational purchase process involves numerous stages. Each stage may involve multiple individuals within the organization and there may not be any one person who is involved at every stage of the process. It is important then for marketers to understand not only the process, but also who is involved at each stage and how they influence the decision. Webster and Wind have identified 12 stages in the purchase process:

1. Identification of needs
2. Establishing product specifications
3. Searching for alternatives
4. Establishing contact with vendors/suppliers
5. Setting purchase and usage criteria
6. Evaluating alternative buying actions
7. Determining the available budget
8. Evaluating specific alternatives
9. Negotiating with suppliers
10. Buying
11. Using
12. Post-purchase evaluation.[3]

These 12 stages need not occur in the order listed and, for some purchase situations, certain stages may be omitted. When selling to organizations, it is particularly critical to understand where it is in the purchase process. An organization that has already identified its needs, set purchase criteria, and evaluated different buying actions (lease vs. purchase, for example) is unlikely to be receptive to efforts to redefine its needs. On the other hand, a firm just beginning to struggle with a problem may be delighted to have assistance with need identification and definition.

Point to Ponder

Are there specific marketing actions that would be more useful for each stage in the organizational buying process? What marketing activities are likely to be most effective at each stage?

Firms frequently employ one of two general purchasing strategies. They may attempt to "simultaneously scan" all potential vendors, or they may first rank vendors according to some criterion, then proceed through a "sequential evaluation" process.[4] The simultaneous scanning process is one in which all vendors are considered at the same time. This process is most likely to occur where there are relatively few vendors, expenditures for the purchase are apt to be large, the probability that vendors cannot meet specifications is high, and management is willing to devote substantial time and resources to the purchase process itself. Many new buying tasks are characterized by this process. In a sequential evaluation process, vendors are reviewed one at a time until one is found acceptable. This may mean that the first supplier considered will be selected. Many rebuy situations are characterized by this process. Sequential evaluation is most likely to occur where product costs are low, management does not wish to devote substantial resources to the purchase process, and there is little risk that a supplier will fail to meet product specifications.

Environmental Factors Affecting the Purchase Process

A number of environmental factors may influence an organization's purchasing behavior. These factors may be external, or they may be a part of the internal environment of the organization. Webster and Wind identify six major external factors that influence the organization:[5]

(a) Physical factors such as climate and distance between the firm and its suppliers
(b) Technological factors, such as the rapidity of change in product technologies
(c) Economic factors, such as interest rates and relative supply and demand for particular products
(d) Political factors, such as trade quotas
(e) Legal factors, such as restrictions on the use of certain types of raw materials
(f) Cultural factors, such as the perceived value of innovation or of time-saving goods

Internal environmental factors that affect the purchase activity of a firm include procurement rules and procedures. These factors may also include the firm's organizational structure, whether it is centralized or decentralized, and its internal "culture," that is, its attitudes toward risk and innovation.

The Buying Center

The key to understanding the purchasing activity of an organization is knowing its buying center. The buying center is that set of individuals who are responsible for the purchase of a particular product within the organization. The buying center may be virtual with individuals contributing to purchase decisions without ever meeting or even interacting with one another. The buying center for a particular product is seldom a part of the formal organization. Rather, the buying center exists for the purpose of solving a certain problem. Buying centers appear and disappear as problems and purchase decisions are resolved. Some members of the organization may play a role in many buying centers, while others may be involved in only one. Some individuals may play multiple roles in any given buying center, while others may be limited to a single role.

Different products may have different buying centers since a number of different individuals may influence the purchase decision and the individuals involved may change from purchase to purchase. In some cases, particularly simple or rebuy situations, the buying center may consist of only one person. More often, however, it includes many individuals playing a variety of roles. One key role in the buying center is that of *gatekeeper*. The gatekeeper controls the flow of information to other members of the buying center. This is frequently accomplished by screening vendors and product information.

Even when the gatekeeper has no direct responsibility for the actual purchase decision, he or she can exert a tremendous influence on the outcome of the purchase process. Vendors and products that are screened out before reaching the decision makers are never considered. Thus, it is critical to the marketer to understand who the gatekeeper is for particular purchases. In many cases, the gatekeeper is the purchasing agent. In some cases, the gatekeeper may be a technical expert. In still other cases, a receptionist or secretary may be the gatekeeper. The marketer must either make an ally of the gatekeeper or find a way around this person into the buying center. The latter approach may be risky, however, since it may arouse antagonism in the gatekeeper.

Other roles in the buying center may also exist:

- *Initiators*, for example, are responsible for identifying the need for a particular product or service. Initiators are typically in or near a user department where the product or service is used.
- *Influencers* and advisors are not directly involved in the purchase decision but do provide opinions and information. These individuals may be technical experts, such as engineers, or they may simply be users.
- *Users* of the product or service may or may not directly influence the purchase decision yet may still have an impact

on the purchase process. The characteristics of the user may also influence the choice of the product. Products considered too complex or dangerous for a particular user group may be eliminated from consideration.

- *Liaisons* and monitors are concerned with expediting the flow of information between members of the buying center and the buying center and vendors. They also see that the process remains in place and moves toward final resolution.
- *Deciders* are individuals who actually make the decision about which product to purchase. They may determine the actual specification for the product, the vendor, or method of sourcing (single vs. multiple vendor). Since there are any number of decisions involved in a purchase, there may be numerous deciders.
- *Authorities* use expertise or power related to the purchase. Senior management often takes this role, approving the decisions of others.

An especially important individual in any organization is the "*linking pin*." Likert has defined a linking pin as an individual who exerts influence in his own group and at higher levels within the organization.[6] Wind and Robertson found evidence of the importance of the linking pin in a study of hospital purchasing.[7] They found that chief radiologists wielded influence in their own departments and with senior hospital administrators. Identifying linking pins is an important activity for the marketer, since communication with, and persuasion of, these key individuals is highly effective in influencing the outcome of the purchase process.

Many factors influence the actions of the buying center and the outcome of the organizational purchasing process. Among these factors are the prices of the product alternatives, the dependability of supply,

---

Point to Ponder

How would a salesperson's presentation, approach, and relationship differ across the many roles within the buying center? Can one salesperson fill all of these roles?

the desire to avoid risk, the organizational structure, social relationships, and buyer–seller communications. The relative importance of each factor depends on the nature of the purchase.

Communications

A key factor in the behavior of organizations is communication. Firms frequently exchange information about products and vendors. It is not unusual for an organization considering the purchase of a product to make numerous inquiries about product alternatives, suppliers, and manufacturers. This word-of-mouth communication among organizational consumers, both within the same organization and across different organizations, is supplemented by information from sales personnel, advertising, and trade shows. Each of these sources of information may reach different members of the buying center. It is critical then that a marketer orchestrate the communications program so that all members of the buying center receive the same message. Equally important however is the packaging of the message in a form that can be readily understood by particular members of the buying center and that addresses the key concerns of each member. An advertisement designed to communicate a product quality message targeted at engineering personnel would be quite different from an advertisement targeted at a nontechnical user, for example.

The Purchasing Agent

As discussed earlier in this chapter, there are many roles within the organizational buying center. Such roles may vary with the type of purchase and type of product and are frequently informal and transient. However, one role in organizational purchasing tends to be defined as a part of the formal organizational structure. This is the purchasing agent. The purchasing agent plays an important role in many different organizational purchases, although this role may change from product to product and organization to organization. Purchasing agents frequently serve as gatekeepers, screening vendors and suppliers for further consideration. They are also likely to be buyers (or implementers), liaisons, and monitors.

It is the responsibility of the purchasing agent to see that the purchase process is concluded (even if the conclusion is not to purchase). The backgrounds and responsibilities of purchasing agents have changed considerably in recent years. Purchasing agents, who in the past were frequently little more than clerks, have become increasingly more professional. Technical training and advanced degrees are common today, and it is not unusual for large firms to have purchasing agents specializing in different types of purchases. For example, one large manufacturer has several specialists whose primary activity is the purchase of fuel coal.

An understanding of the role of the purchasing agent is critical to the marketer's success. The agent who is only a gatekeeper may be approached in a different way from the agent who is also a decider. Purchasing agents frequently perceive their role as one of "watchdog" for the organization. In this role, they seek to assure the firm is getting the best quality product at the lowest price. Purchasing agents are, in fact, simultaneously occupying multiple roles. They have a role relationship with their own organization, and they must interact with numerous divisions within their own organization. Thus, they often occupy several different and potentially conflicting roles even within their own organization. They also are involved in role relationships with each vendor or potential vendor. Thus, there is considerable potential for the development of role stress, role conflict, and role ambiguity. This fact has only recently been recognized, but it is clear that the more clearly the purchasing agent's role is defined, often through formal purchasing procedures, the more satisfied the purchasing agent is in his or her job and the more effective the agent is in negotiations, as measured by savings obtained for the firm. Marketing strategies that serve to reduce role stress will be more successful than those that increase it.

The multiple roles that the purchasing agent must play coupled with the involvement of numerous others in the organization who may have different values and occupy different roles, virtually assures that some conflict will arise in all but the most routine of purchasing activities. Thus, a critical factor in the organizational purchasing process is the way conflict is resolved.

Conflict in Organizational Purchase Decisions

With so many potential contributors to a purchase decision, the organizational purchase process is ripe for the creation of conflict. Conflict is a normal part of group decision making, and need not be considered unhealthy, however. Conflicts arise because individuals in the organization have different goals, perceptions, and needs. Production personnel tend to pay much more attention to product quality, durability, and convenience in use than do financial personnel, who may be more concerned with price and terms of the sale. Each has a different role that leads to a greater emphasis on some attributes of a product or service, and lesser emphasis on others.

Three types of conflict may arise in the purchase process.[8] There may be conflicts regarding the capabilities of products, services, or suppliers. Such conflicts are usually resolved as more information is obtained. A second type of conflict involves disagreements on the criteria for evaluation,that is, how much emphasis to place on a particular product or vendor attributes. This type of conflict is most likely to grow from the differences in the objectives of the various departments represented in the buying center. Such conflicts may be resolved by persuasion, compromise, negotiation, or efforts to create a common view of the problem. A third type of conflict arises from differences in personality or style of decision-making. This type of conflict is the most likely to be destructive since it often results in a political process, involving opposing camps within the

---

Point to Ponder

A salesperson who helps resolve conflicts within a customer firm could be viewed as very helpful. What are the risks of such a strategy?

organization. The objectives of the purchase, and the characteristics of product alternatives, are frequently lost in this process. The marketer or salesperson who understands that organizational conflict occurs can often realize a significant competitive advantage. Conflicts regarding capabilities of products and services can often be resolved with the assistance of the salesperson. Thus, even when the immediate sale is lost, the salesperson has the opportunity to create goodwill and solidify a relationship. The marketer might also be able to facilitate resolution of conflicts arising over differences related to the criteria for evaluation. On the other hand, the smart marketer or salesperson will exit quickly when conflicts of personality or style are present within a potential customer organization. Such conflicts represent a no-win situation for the marketer and are generally best left to competitors.

Takeaways

While there is significant overlap in the rules, forces and processes between buyer (organization) and consumer (individual) decision-making, organizational decisions do have some distinct differences of which you need to be aware. For one, organizational purchases are not made by one person. Individual personalities may play some part, but they are much less of a contributing factor. Additionally, the relationship between a buyer and a vendor may be complex. They may be competitors on a certain level while at the same time supporting each other through the buy-sell arrangement.

We can break organization buying into three primary categories, a straight rebuy, a modified re-buy, or a new task. Each presents different challenges for the marketer and the organization. It is important to recognize that when possible an organization will opt for a straight rebuy because modified and new tasks take additional effort. Because of this, the existing vendor holds tremendous weight even if another vendor could offer a better alternative. Understanding how much time and effort a business puts into this can help a marketer. A potential new vendor will need to design marketing strategies and resource allocation around this fact. They need to demonstrate great added value to lure an account away from a competitor.

Twelve stages of organizational decision-making were identified, which sharply contrasts the five stages through which an individual consumer goes. These stages may happen simultaneously or out of order, but they are each at work on various levels and among various people in the organization.

The buying center includes the people responsible for making a buying decision. They are established to find the best solution for a problem. These individuals will likely be in different roles from technical to managerial to research to oversight.

The "gatekeeper" is the person with the organization that has absolute veto power. This person is often an expert on the product or service involved. While the rest of the buying center may evaluate which product or service to buy, this individual gets the final say, but is bound by budget constraints, company goals, and so on. A savvy marketer will figure out who this person is in an attempt to develop a strong partnership to both acquire new business and to retain business with the organization.

Several other roles may exist within the buying center, including, for example, initiators, who identify a need and liaisons who help keep the flow of information open within the buying center. Each of these plays their part and building your marketing strategies around these various roles will help you better connect with the buying center as a whole.

A marketer must also be prepared for conflict within the buying center. The person who is ready with additional information and resolutions to these conflicts will be at a great advantage. This same marketer should be aware that too much conflict creates a no-win situation and they are best served by cutting their losses and moving on.

Notes

1. Hutt and Speh (2003).
2. Ibid.
3. Webster and Wind (1972).
4. Cardozo (1968).
5. Webster and Wind (1972).
6. Likert (1961).
7. Yoram and Robertson (1982, pp. 169–84).
8. Sheth (1973, pp. 50–56).

CHAPTER 7

Learning More About Customers

This chapter, and two that follow, provide an introduction to the identification and use of existing information, sometimes referred to as secondary information. Part of what makes marketing interesting is the enormous variety in buyer behavior. There is a need for constant discovery and creativity in working with buyers. Although a great deal is known about market response to marketing actions and the factors that influence consumers, much of which has been summarized in this book, the reality and challenge for marketers is that every buyer's decision is unique and buyers change over time. Any effort to influence a buyer is countered by factors beyond the control of the marketer and by competitor's actions in the market. This means that the role of the marketer must, by definition, be one of continuous learning and anticipation of the future. This role is part art and part science. It requires analysis and creativity. It requires comfort with hard numbers but also a willingness to accept uncertainty. The complexity of buyer behavior offers a challenge, but it is not an excuse for failing to create for and provide to the firm the best understanding and quantitative estimates of demand in the future. Even when limited resources are available, it is almost always possible to have conversations with customers. There is also an enormous amount of information available about specific markets and customers in those markets.

There are very few genuinely new research questions. Whatever the topic, it is likely that someone or some organization has collected some relevant information. In some cases, this information might provide an immediate and direct answer to a current research question. More often the existing information will provide an important starting point for additional research. Information about a large array of topics is available from numerous sources. Published academic research and government information in the form of reports or raw data addresses a wide range of topics in economics, demography, health care, geography, social behavior, and media use, among others. In addition, there is a vast array of documents and data that have been archived for historical and record keeping purposes. These documents include meeting minutes of government bodies and other organizations, permits obtained from and contracts filed with government entities, voting records, court proceedings, tax records, and a host of other information. There also exists a large and diverse commercial industry devoted to gathering information for specific purposes. This industry consists of survey research firms, media research agencies, consulting firms, think tanks, professional associations, and similar organizations.

Research that makes use of these many pre-existing sources of information is known as secondary analysis, or in the case of information that has been archived for historical or legal reasons, archival research. The reason for the name, secondary analysis, is because the analysis of the information is for a purpose other than that for which the data were originally collected. In contrast to primary research, where a researcher collects information directly relevant to and for the purpose of answering a specific research question, secondary analysis focuses on the use of information that was collected for some other purpose to answer specific questions. The sources of such pre-existing information are known as secondary sources to contrast them with data collection for a specific purpose, or primary research.

Secondary research can also be divided into custom research and syndicated research. Custom research involves secondary analysis that is conducted for one or more specific organizations and circulation of this research is generally limited to the sponsoring organization. On the other hand, some research providers use secondary research, primary research, or both to create data and reports that are available to whoever is willing to pay for the report. This latter type of research is called syndicated research. Many organizations offer syndicated research reports or data ranging from government agencies, like the Census Bureau to commercial organizations that charge a substantial fee for access to the information that they provide. The issues that arise in using and evaluating custom secondary research and syndicated secondary research are similar, but it is important to recognize that some secondary analysis begins with the results of secondary analyses of others.

Secondary Analysis

Secondary analysis involves the use of sources of data and other information collected by others and archived in some form. Secondary information offers relatively quick and inexpensive answers to many questions. Such information may take a variety of forms. It may be little more than a copy of a published report. In some cases, it may involve a repackaging or reanalysis of data. For example, a number of commercial research providers obtain government data, such as that obtained by the Census Bureau, and develop specialized reports, create convenient data access capabilities, or combine data from multiple sources into a single source. Such repackaged research is often sold as syndicated research because it is made available to multiple users. Other syndicated data providers may obtain information from nongovernment sources. For example, several commercial research providers obtain electronic scanner information from retailers and package it to provide reports on the sales, prices, and other features of retail products for retailers and manufacturers.

Points to Ponder

Where do you find the most reliable and valuable sources of data for secondary analysis? Have you encountered any pros or cons related to working with this data? How have you been able to supplement this data to make it more useable for your business?

In contrast to research providers who offer only secondary research, where data and information are obtained from other sources, a significant segment of this industry consists of organizations that collect their own information and make it available, often at a price, to other organizations. For example, some commercial research providers collect information about product awareness and preference and customer satisfaction for entire industries and sell reports of this research to other organizations. While these firms are themselves engaged in primary research, the users of the information to whom they provide are engaged in secondary analysis. Similarly, some organizations offer reports of large-scale tracking studies of media usage habits, lifestyles, and eating habits and health related behavior. Such research would be considered primary research by the provider but represents secondary research to users because they did not materially participate in the design and analysis of the research.

Advantages and Disadvantage of Secondary Analysis

Like most research tools and methods secondary analysis has both advantages and disadvantages. Secondary research and analysis generally offers a faster and less expensive means for obtaining information than would be the case if a researcher were to undertake primary research. Because data and reports are already available, they can be obtained within days, hours and in the age of the Internet, often within minutes. Because the cost of data collection and reporting has already been covered, or, in the case of syndicated research can be shared by all of the organizations that might be interested, secondary research tends to be less expensive than comparable data obtained through primary research. On the other hand, secondary research may not provide the specific information required for a given purpose and, it may not be as timely as data that are obtained in response to an immediate question.

Secondary analysis can also provide a useful starting point for additional research by suggesting problem formulations, research hypotheses, and research methods. Secondary analysis can also increase the efficiency of research expenditures by identifying significant gaps in knowledge. Secondary analysis may also provide a useful tool for making comparisons. New data may be compared to existing data for purposes of examining differences or trends. It may also provide a basis for determining whether new information is representative of a population, as in the case of sampling. Comparison of the demographic characteristics of a sample to those of a larger population, as specified by the Census Bureau, may reveal how representative the sample is of the larger population.

On the other hand, there are very significant disadvantages associated with secondary analysis, at least for some purposes. The underlying data may not address the research question of interest. Even if the data do address the research question of interest in a general way, the way in which the data were collected, the manner in which variable were defined, or the sample from which the data were obtained may not be appropriate for the research question. If data collection, variable definition, and the sample are appropriate the passage of time may make the data less relevant for an immediate research question.

The Complementarity of Secondary and Primary Research

In most research situations primary and secondary research are used in a complementary fashion, rather than as substitutes for one another. Research efforts generally begin with a question or set of objectives. These objectives are met, and the question answered through the acquisition of information. The source of the information—whether it is secondary source or primary research—is really not important as long as the information is trustworthy and answers the question at hand. In fact, it will be less expensive and time-consuming to use secondary sources. Frequently, however, at least some of the questions at hand have not been answered by prior research; answering these questions requires primary research. In these cases, secondary research helps define the agenda for subsequent primary research by suggesting which questions require answers that have not been obtained in previous research. Secondary data may also identify the means by which the primary research should be carried out:

1. Questions that should be addressed
2. Measurement instruments such as questionnaires and measurement scales
3. Relevant respondent

Where do you find data for secondary analysis? There are many options.

Sources of Secondary Research and Data

There are many sources of secondary data and reports. Often overlooked in the quest for customer information is the data the organization collects as a part of carrying out its routine business. Such information includes sales data, website visits, and other operational data. Table 7.1 lists some potential sources of customer information that may be obtained from or built into routine operations of an organization. Of course, such information must be captured and analyzed, but it is relatively inexpensive to do so.

Online searches using Google, Bing, or other search engines often reveal many relevant sources. There are also specialized online vendors that provide access to and search capabilities for locating secondary sources relevant to particular research questions. An example of such a

Table 7.1 Common sources of customer information within the organization

- Customer service interactions such as call center interactions and chat records, and complaint records
- Customer and/or partner advisory councils
- Internal information such as financial and operational data
- Purchasing data or product usage data
- Transactional and/or relationship surveys data
- Social media, online communities, and website data
- Input documented from frontline employees and sales personnel

commercial vendor is *Proquest* (http://proquest.com/en-US/), which allows a researcher to search nearly 3,000 worldwide business periodicals that cover business and economic conditions, management techniques, theory, and practice of business, advertising, marketing, economics, human resources, finance, taxation, and computers, and among others. Such sites typically require a subscription or charge users per search.

In contrast, there are websites that provide access to social science research, including research papers not yet published, that do not charge for a search or charge a nominal fee. One example of the latter is the social science research network (SSRN) electronic library, which is composed of a number of specialized research networks in the social sciences. Topics covered by networks include accounting, economics, financial economics, legal scholarship, and management (including negotiation and marketing). The SSRN eLibrary consists of an abstract database containing abstracts of scholarly working papers and forthcoming papers, and an electronic paper collection of downloadable full text documents in pdf format. Access to the database and collection is free; some services may require registration or fees.[1] Barker, Barker, and Pinard provide a useful and highly accessible introduction to the use of the Internet as a tool for finding information, as well as the limitations and cautions that go hand in hand with an open and largely unregulated medium like the Internet.[2]

There are a number of "meta-sites" online that provide a large array of links to other sites. Some of these sites are accessible without cost while others require a subscription or fee. These sites differ with respect to their focus, scope, and attention to the quality of information available in the linked sites. There are, in fact many such sites. Table 7.2 provides a listing of some of the more representative broad-based meta-sites.

Table 7.2 Representative meta-sites for finding secondary sources in marketing and the social sciences

- **Data and Information Services Center** (http://disc.wisc.edu/): Provides links to more than 700 searchable online data sources, including government and nongovernment sources. This site is maintained by the University of Wisconsin, Madison. Online links are related to economics, demographics, politics, education, health, education, history, sociology and geography, among others. Includes both United States and International sources

(Continued)

Table 7.2 (Continued)

• **Econdata.Net** (http://econdata.net/): This site, which is sponsored by the U. S. Economic Development Administration is designed to be a first stop for researchers who need demographic, social, and economic information at the state and sub-state level
• **Intute** (http://intute.ac.uk/): A catalog of thousands of searchable websites in the social sciences and other disciplines. Hosted by a consortium of universities in the United Kingdom this site is an outstanding source of high quality international information. This site includes links to sources related to agriculture, business and management, communications, the creative and performing arts, education, law, medicine, engineering and the physical sciences, as well as the social sciences
• **Lexis-Nexis** (http://lexisnexis.com/): Like ProQuest, Lexis-Nexis is a commercial database for which a subscription is required. Lexis-Nexis provides links to legal literature, including judicial decisions, as well as information relevant to for business and market analyses, selected academic literature and government reports, and data sets related to demographic and economic variables
• **Population Reference Bureau** (http://prb.org/): A website that provides summaries of information, including charts, maps, rankings, and graphs for a wide array of demographic, social, health, economic, environmental, and family structure data for the United States and the world. This site also includes teaching resources, including lesson plans and teaching guides, for use in designing course modules using such data
General sources of government data
• **United States Census Bureau** (http://census.gov): This general website for the Census Bureau provides links to reports, data summaries, and raw data for all of the Censuses conducted by the Bureau including the Decennial Census and the several Economic Censuses. The site also provides links to the *American Community Survey*, and ongoing survey that provides annual data about a wide array of population characteristics, and to the population estimates program, which provides estimates of population statistics between censuses
• **FedStats** (http://fedstats.gov): A well-organized source of statistical information available from over 100 U.S. government agency sites. Includes links to information on agricultural production, health care, industries, crime and judicial data, education, energy, labor force, housing, poverty, children, aging populations, and tax returns, among others
• **Stat-USA/Internet** (http://stat-usa.gov/): A website provided by the U.S. Department of Commerce. It is designed to be a single point of access to information about business, trade, and economics from across Federal Government Agencies
• **EDGAR** (http://sec.gov/edgar.shtml): Maintained by the securities and exchange commission, this website is a repository for the filing of annual and quarterly reports by all publicly traded corporations in the United States. A good source of information about individual companies
• **United Nations Statistics Division** (http://unstats.un.org/unsd/default.htm): The United Nations serves as a repository for social, economic, population, energy, crime environment, geographic, and health care data from countries around the world. It also provides an online gateway to statistics relevant to its member nations (http://data.un.org/)

Selected online sources of health and human services information
• **National Center for Health Statistics** (http://cdc.gov/nchs/): The National Center for Health Statistic's website, operated by the Center for Disease Control provides a deep and diverse portal for information about health and health care. Health statistics provided on this site include information related to the health status of the population, experiences with the health care system, enumeration of health problems, the impact of health policies, and trend in health care delivery systems
• **World Health Organization** (http:/who.int/research/en/): The most comprehensive guide to world health. This website includes worldwide national statistics for 70 core indicators on mortality, morbidity, risk factors, service coverage, and health systems, data on chronic diseases and their risk factors for all WHO Member States, standardized data and statistics for infectious diseases at country, regional, and global levels, and links to local and region information of member nations
• **National Center for Educational Statistics** (http://nces.ed.gov/): The National Center for Education Statistics (NCES) is the United States agency with primary responsibility for collecting and analyzing data related to education. This website includes information on a wide array of education issues including reports and raw data
• **Child Trends Databank** (http://childtrendsdatabank.org/): The Child Trends website is maintained by a nonprofit research organization dedicated to providing research and data to inform decision-making that affects children
• **Department of Health and Human Service Gateway to Data and Statistics** (http://hhs-stat.net/): Designed to complement other U.S. government data resources, this website provides links to academic research, government reports, and databases related to health, poverty, special populations, and family and community services
Representative commercial and nonprofit sources of secondary information
• **Simmons** (https://simmonsresearch.com/solutions/) powered by the industry renowned National Consumer Study. This high quality, nationally representative study is the result of a comprehensive, continuously fielded survey of approximately 25,000 U.S. adults, including over 7,500 English—and Spanish-speaking Hispanics. The National Consumer study continuously measures consumer attitudes, product and brand preferences, media consumption habits, and demographic and lifestyle characteristics
• **Easy Analytic Software, Inc.** (http://easidemographics.com/index.asp): A commercial data provider that organizes demographic data by geography and life stage cluster. Information includes data from Mediamark Research, which includes comprehensive demographic, lifestyle, product usage, and media exposure to all forms of advertising media collected from a single sample of more than 26,000 households
• **Roper Center for Public Opinion Research** (http://ropercenter.uconn.edu/): This Center, which is housed at the University of Connecticut, is one of the largest archives of social science data, with particular emphasis on data from public opinion surveys. Data date from the 1930s, when survey research was in its infancy, to the present. Most of the data are related to the United States, but over 50 nations are represented in the archives

(Continued)

Table 7.2 (Continued)

• **The Economist Intelligence Unit** (http://eiu.com/index.asp?rf=0): The Economist Intelligence Unit provides a constant flow of information, data, analysis, and forecasts related to social, economic, demographic, and political variables on more than 200 countries and six key industries
• **A. C. Nielsen** (http://nielsen.com/): Nielsen is one of the largest providers of data on product purchase and use, retail sales, media use, online, and mobile telephone use, and other information about consumer behavior. Data and reports available for much of the world. Offers Nielsen Scholastic Services, which provides programs, data, curriculum materials, and other resources for faculty members and students
• **IMS** (http://imshealth.com/portal/site/imshealth/): IMS is one of the largest commercial providers of information about health care and health care products. IMS provides worldwide data on the sale and prescription of pharmaceutical products and medical devices, on disease and treatment patterns, and industry trends
• **eMarketer** (https://emarketer.com). Data and analysis on e-business, Internet marketing, and technology trends. Includes news, analysis, charts, reports, and information on products, as well as statistics through eStat database
• **Mintel Reports** (http://mintel.com): As a globally recognized market analyst, Mintel produces some 600 reports into European, UK-specific, and US consumer markets every year. There are global reports, as well as extensive industry/market research for China and Australia
• **Euromonitor Passport** (http://go.euromonitor.com/passport_.html): provides international market intelligence, including economic statistics, on industries, countries, and consumers

Government Sources of Information

Some of the most reliable and comprehensive sources of secondary data are government sources. Much of the data provided by the United States Government is collected by the Census Bureau, which employs very elaborate quality controls. Although best known for its work on the Decennial Population Census, which occurs every ten years, the Census Bureau conducts a wide array of other censuses and surveys. It is also the primary collector of data for many other government agencies, such as the Bureau of Labor Statistics.

One of the larger sectors of the United States economy and an area of significant research activity in the social sciences and other fields is health and human services. The United States government as well as many other state and local governments and commercial organizations collect and disseminate an enormous amount of information and data regarding health and disease, health related behaviors, quality of life, and human development.

Commercial and Not-for-Profit Information Providers

In today's information driven economy there is a huge commercial industry involved in the collection, analysis, and reporting of information for various purposes. Much of this data of very high quality and is used by businesses and policy makers for decision-making. However, such data also can and has been used to address important basic research questions and to test theories. While much of this type of data is available only for a fee, commercial providers often have programs for providing access to their data to academic researchers and students. In addition, various not-for-profit centers maintain data sources and will often provide access to the data for no or a modest cost.

The various secondary data sources listed in Table 7.2 are by no means a comprehensive listing. Rather they are intended to provide examples of more general information sources. There are other general source as well, and a huge number of highly specialized sources. Whatever the topic, there is likely to be secondary source of information that can be used as a first point of analysis for a research question. However, whatever the source of the data and the type of analysis to be undertaken, it is important to carefully evaluate the integrity and reliability of the data before proceeding with an analysis.

Not all information obtained is equally reliable or valid. In an Internet age characterized by the presence of "fake news," information must be evaluated carefully and weighted according to its credibility and how recent it was obtained. Fortunately, the same questions that arise in the evaluation of secondary sources also arise in the context of primary research. The only difference is that these questions must be addressed retrospectively in the case of secondary research, while they should be addressed prospectively in the case of primary research. It is also important to recognize that information may simultaneously be valid for drawing some conclusions and invalid for drawing other conclusions. Research is not uniformly valid or invalid; rather, it is only valid or invalid with respect to specific questions.

When evaluating secondary source information six questions must be answered:

1. Why was the study or data collection effort undertaken?
2. Who obtained the information?
3. What information or data was actually collected?
4. During what time period was the information or data collected?
5. By what method(s) was the information or data obtained?
6. How consistent is the information or data with that found in other sources?

In answering these basic questions other, more specific questions will arise. These more specific questions include the source(s) of the data, measures used, the time of data collection, and the appropriateness of analyses and conclusions. Use of these six generic questions can provide a means for assessing the validity of research for any given purpose. The next chapter will consider each of these questions in detail.

Takeaways

Due to the enormous variety of buyer behaviors, constant discovery and creativity are needed but fortunately, considerable information is already available. While, certainly, new data is helpful for identifying changing trends and business-specific behavior, much of buyer behavior is fixed and has been well-studied. Any question you have about buyer behavior that we have not thus far discussed in this book has very likely been studied by someone who collected extensive data on the topic. It is simply a matter of acquiring and analyzing the data to gain new insights and develop new strategies. These data may not stand alone but it gives you a framework on which to develop your own studies. This secondary analysis of pre-existing data helps you understand what new questions need to be asked in order to customize data analysis to your business needs. Utilizing secondary analysis is the cost-effective way to develop and execute data-driven strategies.

There are clear advantages and disadvantages to using secondary analysis. These data are relatively quick and easy to acquire. They may be openly available online or downloadable for a fee. This is in contrast to the time and expense of collecting primary data, which could take months or even years to acquire. Because many entities will be using these data, the cost is shared among the entities. Secondary analysis can help identify and fill in knowledge gaps as well as provide insights into the larger population to which there is no ready access.

On the other hand, these data are often lacking in certain areas. You need specific questions answered and find that the question was not asked. These data are otherwise somehow lacking. In these instances, primary and secondary data complement one another. First, you complete secondary analysis, identifying what data have already been collected. Then you look at what questions were not asked to that you can complete primary analysis separately. Your primary analysis may be less comprehensive, and it may have a less than statistically relevant sample but when combined with the secondary analysis a more complete picture of consumer behavior in your niche begins to take shape.

When you need secondary analysis, time is of the essence. We discussed several places to acquire analysis specific to your industry, but you will find many more as you explore the possibilities. Government sources are a great place to start and there are also many commercial and not-for-profit options.

In this chapter, we very briefly discussed that all data and analysis are not equal. A marketer must be careful. They must not only know that the research firm is reputable; they must understand what the data truly represent. Data can be misleading when they are applied too broadly.

The next chapter will explore how to evaluate secondary analysis to ensure that the information and numbers are reliable and valid.

Notes

1. http://papers.ssrn.com/sol3/DisplayAbstractSearch.cfm
2. Barker, Barker, and Pinard (2010).

CHAPTER 8

Evaluating Secondary Sources of Information About Customers

Identification of sources of information about consumers, some of which were described in the previous chapter, is but the first step in developing an understanding of consumers. Not all information is equally relevant or reliable. This chapter offers a framework for evaluating information.

We like to think that the numbers never lie but we know that in practical application that simply is not true. Every savvy marketer recognizes that some statistics and studies must be taken with a grain of salt. Their sample size was not statistically significant. The data collected are too niche. The data were collected to prove a theory or justify a pre-determined course of action.

There are many reasons to be suspicious of data, but this is no reason to throw the "baby out with the bathwater." You can acquire reasonable certainty that secondary analysis will be helpful to you. You simply need to ask the right questions.

Let us consider specific questions for which you need answers in order to know that a specific source of secondary analysis is worth your time and money.

Why Was the Study or Data Collection Effort Undertaken?

Information is rarely collected without some intent. The intent of a particular data collection effort significantly influences the data collected and findings produced by any analysis. Data collected to further the interests of a particular group or organization are especially suspect. For example, the results of a survey reported by a lobbyist organization seeking support for a particular policy position is likely to be less objective than results of research carried out by a neutral third party. If an organization's funding is dependent on the outcome of the report, the data slanted.

Unfortunately, it is not always easy to determine when vested interests have influenced the design of prior research. Even when researchers are more neutral it is possible for biases and frames of reference to influence research outcomes. The degree of precision, the types of classifications or categories used, and the method by which data are collected and reported are often dictated by the intent of the study. Thus, in evaluating research, a researcher conducting a secondary analysis must always ask whether the purpose of the study was to reach a pre-determined conclusion or whether the primary researcher was potentially influenced by a strong point-of-view.

Even when data are not collected for purposes of advocating or supporting a particular position, the purpose of a study may confound the interpretation of the data. Consider the following example. The best-known measure of price movements in the United States is the consumer price index (CPI) calculated monthly by the U.S. Bureau of Labor Statistics. This index is based on the prices of about 80,000 items of consumption in more than 200 categories. The price of each item contributing to the index is calculated by surveying urban wage earners and clerical workers in some base year and computing the average price paid for each item.[1] The index represents an average for a representative family of four (father, mother; and two children under the age of 18) living in an urban, but not a rural area.[2] Thus, while the index is a useful point of reference for making comparisons over time, it is not representative of the expenditures of most families. It is only a very rough index of what is happening to purchasing power and is not often useful for specific decisions where a high degree of precision is required or where expenditure patterns are different from those used to define the index.

The purpose of the original data collection effort also has an influence on its credibility. Some data are collected to product "quick and dirty" results intended only to provide direction for decision-making or very rough approximations. Such results may be perfectly appropriate in the context in which the data were collected but may lack the precision or reliability required by other research questions.

Who Obtained the Information?

Information from certain sources may be more credible than information from others. This arises not just from the biases that may be at work, but also from differences in technical competence, resources, and quality. Some organizations have developed reputations for high quality control work and for the integrity of their data. Others have reputations for poor work. Generally, those sources of high integrity will provide sufficient information about how the information was obtained to enable a review of the technical adequacy of the data. Learning about the reputations of various sources of information requires investigating their previous work. Contacting clients and others who have used information supplied by the organization will also provide some indication of the reputation of an organization. One might also examine the training and expertise present in an organization supplying the information.

As noted earlier it is also worthwhile determining whether the organization that sponsored or conducted the research had a vested interest in any particular outcome. For example, an organization that reports a study of its own effectiveness might have a vested interest in accentuating the positive. A rather sizable industry exists to produce what is often called "advocacy research." Such research is not designed to produce unbiased answers to questions. Rather, the research is conducted for the purpose of providing support for a particular conclusion or position. While such research may still yield insights, it must be interpreted with caution.

What Information or Data Was Actually Collected?

In the early 1950s, a Congressional Committee published an estimate of the annual "take" from gambling in the United States. The estimate, $20 billion, was actually picked at random. One committee member was quoted as saying, "We had no real idea of the money spent. The California Crime Commission said $14 billion. Virgil Peterson of Chicago said $30 billion. We picked $20 billion as the balance of the two."[3] This is an example of information entered into the public record that had no empirical basis. No data were collected at all; only a couple of opinions were sought and averaged. "Mythical numbers" are more common than one would wish. These mythical numbers, estimates based on pure guesswork, represent the extreme case, but they serve to emphasize the need for asking what information was actually collected in the primary research effort.

There are frequently big differences in the frequencies with which individuals actually engage in a behavior, as measured by actual observation and counting and self-reported frequencies.[4] This is not just because people want to look better to others by over-reporting socially desirable behaviors and under-weighting undesirable behavior. This certainly happens. However, it is also the case that the limitations of human memory and selective attention biases also distort self-report behavior.[5] This does not mean that self-report data are never useful. Indeed, there are many behaviors that are not easily observed by others and such information as perceptions, preferences, opinions, and attitudes are only accessible by the person that holds them. This volume includes several chapters on self-report and observational data that elaborate on the relative advantages and disadvantages of such data.

The context in which data are collected may also influence the results. Consider a study of consumer preferences that found 60 percent of all consumers preferred Brand A. Such a finding is impressive until one learns that brands B and C, the major competitors of A, were not included on the list from which consumers were to select a product. Voter preferences may appear very different depending on how the question is asked, for example, "do you prefer candidate A to candidate B," vs. "do you approve of candidate A." Relative judgments often produce different results from absolute judgments and relative judgments may differ depending on the point of comparison. However, there are many contexts in which relative judgments are the most useful because they better mirror behaviors of interest. This is especially true in the context of voting behavior and product choices where someone might select the "lesser of evils."

Many of the things researchers wish to measure cannot be observed directly. In such circumstances, it may be possible to obtain an estimate indirectly, by using a surrogate measure that is observable and assumed to be related to the more interesting phenomenon. The critical assumption of such indirect measurement techniques is that there is a relationship between the observable measure and the unobservable event of interest. Even when this assumption is correct, however, the relationship may be decidedly less than perfect. Consider studies of the success of graduates of corporate training programs. Success is difficult to measure because it involves a variety of dimensions and can be measured at many different points in time.

One organization may report results using turnover during the year following completion of the training program. A second organization may use rapidity of advancement within the organization and salary increases over a three-year period. Still another organization may use ratings of success by supervisors after six months on the job.

In each case, the data may be used to relate completion of the training program to success on the job. Yet the relationship reported may vary widely from one study to another. The differences in the findings are attributable to the data that were actually collected not what these data were interpreted to mean. Knowing what information was actually obtained is often very useful for reconciling conflicting results.

Even when direct measurement is possible, the ways in which data are defined and classified may confound the interpretations made. Categorizations and classifications may vary widely, and their relevance and meaning for a particular purpose must always be investigated. For example, what is a family? Is a single, self-supporting person, living alone a family? Are unmarried cohabitants a family?

For some purposes and in some studies the answer is likely to be yes, while in other cases the answer is likely to be no. Apparent inconsistencies across studies often have more to do with the operational definition of terms than the actual differences in the underlying phenomena. Of course, such problems hinder the effective comparison of results across studies and therefore affect the generalizability of conclusions that can be drawn from secondary analysis.

During What Time Period Was the Information or Data Collected?

In a study of the perception of the price of mobile telephone service, it was found that consumers were very much aware of the price of calls and very sensitive to even small price hikes. The results of the study might be interpreted as an indication that consumers are very price sensitive. The study, however, was carried out while an intense, highly publicized debate over telephone prices raged, a debate that included several prominent politicians involved in a political campaign. It is likely that the results of the study would have been different had the study been carried out when there was less publicity about telephone prices.

Time is an important factor to be considered when evaluating information. As in the example above, factors present at the time of information collection may influence the results obtained. Time may also influence the definition of measures. For example, in the context of retailing activity when is a sale made? Does the sale occur upon the placement of an order, receipt of the order, time of shipment, time of delivery, date of billing, date of payment, or the date payment is actually recorded? Are returned items, which can account for 20 percent of all sales in some product categories, included or excluded in the measurement of sales. Different accounting systems place emphasis on different points in time and produce differences in information. Shifts in the point of time when measurements are taken may have very pronounced effects on the results obtained.

Time may also make information obsolete. Technological changes may change perceptions; lifestyles may change. Sooner or later, most data become obsolete and of interest only for historical purposes. How quickly data become obsolete depends on the type of data, the purpose for which they are used, and changes in the environment over time. The user of secondary information should always know when data were collected, however, particularly since there may be a time lag between data collection and the availability of results.

By What Method(s) Was the Information or Data Obtained?

The quality of any research cannot be evaluated without knowledge of the methodology employed when collecting the data. This is no less true of secondary data. Information about the size and nature of samples, response rates, experimental procedures, validation efforts, question-naires, interview guides or protocols, and analytic methods should be available in sufficient detail to allow a knowledgeable critique of the data collection procedure. For example, it has become fashionable for many periodicals to publish questionnaires for readers to complete and return.

The responses are then complied and reported in the publication. While these surveys may make entertaining reading, it is not clear to whom the results apply. How are readers of particular publications different from the general population? One would certainly expect very different responses on certain topics from readers of *Playboy* and readers of the *Christian Science Monitor*. It is not even reasonable to generalize such results to all readers of the magazine; the people who elect to respond may differ from those who did not. Many organizations report results of surveys of their customers or clients. Such surveys may be quite useful but indicate nothing about individuals or organizations that are not customers or clients.

If observations of behavior or activity are reported, who did the observation and under what circumstances? Are the data based solely on human observation or is there a written or electronic record? How representative were the circumstances under which the observations occurred? Was there potential for the very act of observation to influence the outcomes? For example, in evaluating classroom-teaching performance were the teacher and students aware that the observation was occurring? Did the teacher have prior notice of the observation, which might have provided an opportunity for preparation that might not otherwise be typical?

The question of sampling and sample design, how people are selected for participation in a survey, is a critical issue for the evaluation of survey data because it deals with the question of the generalizability of results. It is also important to determine who responded and the response rate. A survey with a response rate of 80 percent is certainly more credible than one with a 5 percent response rate, all else being equal. Given that a result was obtained in a particular study, can that result be considered representative of some larger population? What is the nature of that population? All too frequently in examining secondary data it is impossible to identify that larger population. A description of the

---

Point to Ponder

There are many Internet sites that provide product and service reviews offered by consumers. What factors would you consider in determining whether such reviews are credible?

sampling procedure is always necessary when evaluating the usefulness of data. For example, suppose that it was reported by an independent research firm that 60 percent of subjects given a choice between a charter school and a traditional public school selected the charter school. This result is impressive for the charter school but becomes questionable if it were determined that all of those sampled lived in an area with a high number of students enrolled in the charter school.

How Consistent Is the Information or Data with that Found in Other Sources?

When information obtained from multiple independent sources is consistent, confidence in that information is increased. Whether evaluating data obtained from secondary sources or the results of primary research efforts, the best strategy is to determine the extent to which the information is consistent with information obtained from other sources. Ideally, two or more independent sources should arrive at the same or similar conclusions. When disagreement among sources does exist, it is helpful to try to identify reasons for such differences and to determine which source is more credible. This is not always easy, even with relatively complete information. Nevertheless, careful analysis of the secondary sources may reveal reasons for the inconsistency that lead to greater insights. For example, different measures may have been employed or data may have been obtained at different points in time. On the other hand, when radically different results are reported and little basis for evaluating the information collection procedure is found, it is appropriate to be skeptical of all of the data.

Takeaways

Before investing in secondary analysis, it is important to consider several important points about that data. This chapter discussed questions you should ask about the reports you are considering. Among them are:

- Why was the study or data collection effort undertaken?
- Who obtained the information?

- What information or data was actually collected?
- During what time period was the information or data collected?
- By what method(s) was the information or data obtained?
- How consistent is the information or data with that found in other sources?

By asking these questions and the ones we will discuss in the next chapter, you can better evaluate the strengths and weaknesses of the information. What you find out may lead you to scrap the data altogether or it may act as springboard for further analysis and action.

Notes

1. Greenlees and McClelland (2008, pp. 3–19).
2. Johnson, Rogers, and Tan (2001, pp. 28–45).
3. Singer (1971, p. 410).
4. Gosling et al. (1998, pp. 1337–49).
5. Schwarz and Vaughn (2002).

CHAPTER 9

Analyzing Secondary Customer Data

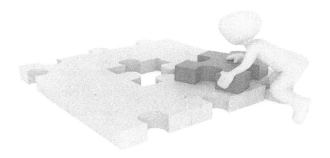

In this chapter, we will describe approaches to the analysis of secondary analysis that you can effectively apply in your own marketing efforts. We will look at different kinds of analyses and how you can put consumer data to work for you.

Archival Data

In the last chapter, we largely focused on the re-analysis of data or research reports originally collected for purposes of research. The original research that gave rise to the data or research report may have had a different purpose than that of the intended secondary analysis, but the process that gave rise to it included a research design that when adequately described provides a basis for evaluating the integrity, relevance, and generalizability of the underlying data and reported results. However, there are many other sources of secondary information that did not originate in a formal research process. Government, corporate and church records, reports and filings, personal correspondence, medical treatment records, minutes of meetings, court records, and genealogical records are all examples of written documents that may be archived and used for secondary analysis. However, archives may also include photographs, video and audio recordings, oral histories, maps, furniture, architectural drawings, and land surveys among others. Indeed, almost any artifact can become the basis for archival research.

While it might seem that archival research is most useful for conducting historical analysis, and a great deal of archival research is of a historical nature, archival data also lend themselves to other types of secondary analyses. For example, a very robust stream of research on the economics and sociology of organizational relationships rests on the secondary analysis of legal contracts.[1] Tax records, which are collected for government record keeping and legal purposes, have been used in secondary analyses to evaluate the effects of different tax policies over time and across different political units on such things as philanthropic giving, entrepreneurial activity, and investment in research and development by corporations. The spectrum of research topics that have been addressed by secondary analysis is very broad and limited only be the imagination and creativity of researchers.

The secondary analysis of archival records and artifacts brings special problems, however. Since the underlying data or artifact was not created by a formal research process there is a need to understand the reasons for its existence as well as why it was saved or survived. The context in which the underlying data were created also is important to understanding its meaning. Authenticating the archival artifact can also be a challenge, especially for such things as personal correspondence, written accounts of events, and even visual media such as photographs.

Analytic Techniques

Secondary analysis can take many forms. Generally, the primary determinants of the analysis are the research question itself and the characteristics of the underlying data. Identifying information relevant to a particular research question is only the first step in secondary analysis.

In an age of instant access to information it is easy to become overwhelmed by information. Finding order and meaning in a plethora of information is often difficult, particularly when there are inconsistencies, omissions, and differences in methods among various sources.

A common problem faced by researchers employing secondary analysis is that of combining the findings and conclusions of several sources of information. The synthesis of information is an important skill and was long criticized for its lack of objectivity.[2]

Secondary analysis can range from simple descriptive reporting of results, to new analyses of underlying data, to efforts to combine different sources of information to construct an answer to a new research question, to efforts to integrate a body of literature to reconcile contradictions and draw conclusions about the presence or absence (and strength) of specific effects or variables. A number of authors have addressed specific approaches to the analysis of secondary sources.[3] The most common approaches to secondary analysis are:

1. descriptive analysis
2. interpretive analysis,
3. comparative analysis
4. verification
5. re-analysis of data
6. integration through analysis of research design and setting (meta-analysis).

We will explore each one in detail.

Descriptive Analysis

Descriptive analysis involves describing the attributes, findings, and conclusions of past research. There is little effort to integrate or interpret the underlying data beyond reporting what was found and perhaps counting or otherwise summarizing various results. For example, a review of surveys of schools undertaken by different researchers that provides the numbers of students with particular special education needs and the number and types of programs offered to such students would be an example of a descriptive analysis.

Interpretive Analysis

In contrast to descriptive analysis, interpretive analysis seeks to go beyond the data or particular set of findings to develop a larger meaning of the underlying data. For example, in the analysis of survey of schools above the secondary analyst might go beyond mere description to related program availability to classroom success and draw conclusions about the relative efficacy of program types. Interpretive analysis is especially common in archival research in which there is a need to place a particular artifact or set of artifacts within a social, cultural, or economic context. Interpretive research often seeks to identify a larger meaning of an artifact by identifying its social or cultural significance and origins.

Comparative Analysis

Comparative analysis focuses on the identification of similarities and differences across sources and data collection efforts. Comparisons may involve analyses of differences over time or among social groups or regions. In such cases comparative analysis may be combined with primary research in a replication or restudy of the original research to follow up the original sample or to make comparisons with additional groups, settings, or circumstances. An example of comparative analysis is found in Di Gropello, who used secondary data to analyze the effects of decentralization of school management in Central America and compare centralized management systems with decentralized management systems.[4] Key conclusions of this analysis, which was sponsored by the World Bank, were that decentralized, school-based management models produce greater community involvement and greater effort on the part of teachers while producing learning outcomes as high as in traditional schools despite being located primarily in the poorest and more isolated areas.

Verification

Verification is similar to comparative analysis but with the more limited objective of substantiating prior results. The prior results provide the point of comparison to which new data are applied. For example, in examining the efficacy of a particular treatment for a psychological disorder, secondary analysis of medical records may demonstrate that efficacy is similar to what had previously been demonstrated in more controlled clinical research.

Re-Analysis

Among the more common types of secondary analysis is re-analysis of the underlying data. Such re-analysis might take the form of applying different analytic tools or the addition new variables obtained from other sources. More often, re-analysis involves asking new questions of the data that are different from the questions that gave rise to the original data collection effort. This involves approaching the data in ways that weren't originally intended by using the data to investigate a different research question, theme, or topic.

Generally, the more in-depth the material, and the more information that exists about the underlying data and how it was obtained, the greater the likelihood that the data's utility for addressing new questions can be evaluated. For example, data originally obtained for purposes of understanding access to health care among lower socio-economic families might be used in secondary analysis to examine the impact of health access and health problems on the educational achievement of children in these families. This might involve the use of data with respect to educational performance obtained in the original study or the combination of data from the health care study with other secondary data related to educational performance.

Finally, in the context of long-term streams of carefully designed research it is often possible to use differences in the research designs of different studies to examine the relative influence of variables that contribute to the obtained outcomes of results. Such meta-analyses involve the statistical analysis of differences and similarities in both the design and results of different studies to identify the degree to which different effects and different design parameters (such as sample or type of measure) explain the pattern of results obtained across studies. There is a rich literature on the technical details of conducting meta-analysis.[5] The chapters in this volume on meta-synthesis and meta-analysis also provide useful introductions and more technical information about performing such informative analyses.

Ultimately, the type of secondary analysis that a researcher carries out must be dictated by the research question. In many applied contexts a very simple descriptive analysis may be sufficient. In other situations, the research question may require integration across studies and sources but not at highly quantified and specific level. Secondary analysis that focuses on the testing and development of theory may require the quantitative precision of meta-analysis.

Point to Ponder

Think about a market or group of consumers about which you would like to know more. What sources might you consult for more information and how might you put the information together to tell a story that provides an understanding of these consumers?

Takeaways

Secondary analysis and archival research are very common in both academic research in the social sciences and in applied research designed to address practical policy and business question. The prudent user of such information will know what information is relevant for a given situation and will select an appropriate source of information. Once you have acquired the research for secondary research, you will take it through one or more forms of analysis. The one you choose largely depends on your purpose for the data. After analyzing the secondary data, you'll have a clearer picture of what additional questions you need to ask through your own research in order to practically apply what you have learned.

Notes

1. MacNeil (1978, pp. 854–905).
2. Glass (1977).
3. Stewart and Kamins (1993); Smith (2008); Bulmer, Sturgis, and Allum (2009).
4. Di Gropello (2006).
5. Cooper (2008).

CHAPTER 10

Conclusion

This chapter provides a summary of the links between consumer behavior and marketing planning and action. An understanding of consumer behavior is a prerequisite for managing the marketing function, as well as the business as a whole. A marketer's responsibility is to understand consumer behavior so that he or she can influence that behavior through the design of products, services, and marketing programs that match the goals and preferences of consumers. In this way, marketers add value to the organizations for which they work, increase customer satisfaction, and improve the quality of life in a society. Individual consumers and business buyers alike purchase goods and services to meet specific goals. When these goals are known, there is a better understand why people buy what they buy. These goals always exist but their links to purchase behavior may not always be straightforward. Even what seems like a very simple purchase may be the result of a complex process that is influenced by many factors.

Consumers and buyers are influenced by many forces—cultural, social, and psychological. However, it is important for us to give credit

> ## Point to Ponder
>
> What does it mean that consumers influence marketing actions more than marketing actions influence consumers? What does this suggest about how marketers should do their job?

where credit is due. Consumers are not sheep being idly guided. They make conscious decisions in pursuit of goals. Indeed, it is usually the case that consumers influence marketing actions more than marketing actions influence consumers.

To understand consumer behavior, we must not only understand the goals of consumers, but also how these influences impact their decisions. These decisions are influenced by things like past experiences and emotions that shape how they see products and services. Part of what makes marketing challenging, and interesting at the same time, is the fact that consumers differ from one another and the same consumer can be different at different points in time and in different situations. While all purchases of consumers and buyers involve distinct decision-making process, that process is often not the same for all consumers or all products. Every consumer's purchase involves a journey, but that journey can be very different from one consumer to another.

Success as a marketer and success in business requires the development of a deep understanding of the consumer and his or her journey during the purchase and consumption processes. There is never an excuse for failure to develop such an understanding. Even the most resource constrained marketers and businesses can have conversations with customers. Even in the absence of the ability to conduct sophisticated and expensive marketing research, the marketer has access to information about the consumers with whom the business does business. There is also an enormous amount of information about consumers that is readily available at little or no cost.

Peter Drucker argued that: "*There is only one valid definition of business purpose:* **to create a customer**. *... Because its purpose is to create a customer, the business enterprise has two—and only two—basic functions: marketing and innovation. Marketing and innovation produce results; all the rest are 'costs'.*" This is the reason that consumer behavior lies at the heart of modern marketing. The successful marketer is one who effectively develops products and brands that are of value to consumers, and who effectively presents these products and brands to consumers in appealing and persuasive ways. One essential reason for studying consumer behavior is to enable marketing managers to make better marketing decisions while reducing the incidence of product failures. However, it is more complicated than that.

Marketing is a complex activity, requiring systematic analysis, financial evaluation, and business judgment. It also requires inspiration and creativity, thus demanding quite diverse talents seldom found in a single individual. In this sense, marketing can be thought of as a group activity or a group process.

It is vital that marketing decisions be data-driven but collecting and analyzing data as an organization can be time-consuming and costly. Fortunately, secondary research helps reduce these costs. By acquiring secondary data from the firm's own operating environment or from third parties, the marketer can not only acquire much-needed data faster and more affordably, it can use these data as a springboard to determine what additional data needs exist for informing decisions.

The successful marketing manager, who is responsible for analyzing, forecasting, planning, and overseeing the execution and evaluation of the marketing plan is a business person. He or she is a decision maker, business trained and profit oriented. Infrequently is a marketing manager a creative genius. Yet creative inspiration is the spark that fires the marketing effort, transforming a marketing plan from a lifeless document into a driving, dynamic achievement. Knowledge of consumer behavior is what gives marketing both its brain and its heart.

Point to Ponder

What do you think of Drucker's view that marketing and innovation are the only two basic functions of business? How do marketing and innovation complement one another?

Note

1. Drucker (1974, p. 61).

References

Bulmer, M.I., P. Sturgis, and N. Allum. 2009. *The Secondary Analysis of Survey Data*. London: Sage.

Denove, C., and J.D. Power IV. 2006. *Satisfaction: How Every Great Company Listens to the Voice of the Customer*. New York, NY: Portfolio.

Nelson, P. March/April, 1974. "Advertising as Information." *Journal of Political Economy* 82, pp. 311–29.

Smith, E. 2008. *Using Secondary Data in Educational and Social Research. Maidenhead Berkshire*, UK: Open University Press.

Bagozzi, R.P., and U. Dholakia. 1999. "Goal Setting and Goal Striving in Consumer Behavior." *Journal of Marketing* 63 (Special Issue: Fundamental Issues and Directions for Marketing), pp. 19–32.

Barker, D.I., M. Barker, and K.T. Pinard. 2010. *Internet Research—Illustrated*, 5th ed. Florence, KY: Course Technology.

Berning, C., A. Kohn, and J.Jacoby. September, 1974. "Patterns of Information Acquisition in New Product Purchases." *Journal of Consumer Research* 1, pp. 18–22.

Best, A., and A.R. Andreason. 1976. *Talking Back to Business: Voiced and Unvoiced Consumer Complaints*. Washington, DC: Center for Study of Responsive Law.

Bettman, J. 1979. *Information Processing Theory of Consumer Choice*. Boston: Addison Wesley, Longman.

Bettman, J.R., and C.W. Park. 1980. "Effects of Prior Knowledge and Experience and Phase of Choice Process on Consumer Decision Processes: A Protocol Analysis." *Journal of Consumer Research* 7, pp. 234–48.

Buck, R. 1988. *Human Motivation and Emotion*, New York, NY: Wiley.

Cardozo, R.N. 1968. "Segmenting the Industrial Market." *Proceedings of the American Marketing Association's Fall Conference*. Chicago: American Marketing Association.

Claritas 2018. "My Best Segments, Segment Details." https://segment ationsolutions.nielsen.com/mybestsegments/Default.jsp?ID=30&menuOption =segmentdetails&pageName=Segment%DEtails

Claxton, J.D., J.N. Fry, and B. Portis. December, 1974. "A Taxonomy of Prepurchase Information Gathering Patterns." *Journal of Consumer Research* 1, pp. 35–42.

Cooper, H.M. 2008. *Research Synthesis and Meta-analysis: A Step-by-Step Approach*, 4th ed. Thousand Oaks, CA: Sage.

Cort, S.G., and L.G. Dominguez. May, 1977. "Cross-Shopping and Retail Growth." *Journal of Marketing Research* 14, pp. 187–92.

Dewey, J. 1910. *How We Think*. Lexington, MA: D.C. Heath.

Di Gropello, E. 2006. "A Comparative Analysis of School-Based Management in Central America." World Bank Working Paper No. 72. Washington, DC: World Bank.

Drucker, P.F. 1974. *Management: Tasks, Responsibilities, Practice*, 61. London: William Heinemann Ltd.

Eagly, A.H., and S. Chaiken. 1993. *The Psychology of Attitudes*. Orlando, FL: Harcourt Brace Jovanovich, Inc.

Fishbein, M., and I. Ajzen. 1975. *Belief, Attitude, Intention and Behavior: An Introduction to Theory and Research*, 6. Boston: Addison-Wesley; See also, Ajzen, I. 2005. *Attitudes, Personality and Behavior*, 2nd ed. Maidenhead, UK: Open University Press.

For more information see Li, Y.2005. *Structure and Evolution of Chinese Social Stratification*. Lanham, MD: University Press of America.

Furse, D., G. Punj, and D.W. Stewart. March, 1984. "A Typology of Individual Search Strategies Among Purchasers of New Automobiles." *Journal of Consumer Research* 10, pp. 417–31.

Glass, G.V. 1977. *Integrating Findings: The Meta-analysis of Research*. Beverly Hills, CA: Sage.

Gosling, S.D., O.E. John, R.W. Robins, and K.H. Craik. 1998. "Do People Know How They Behave? Self-Reported Act Frequencies Compared with On-Line Codings by Observers." *Journal of Personality and Social Psychology* 74, pp. 1337–49.

Greenlees, J.S., and R.B. McClelland. 2008. "Addressing Misconceptions about the Consumer Price Index." *Monthly Labor Review* 131, pp. 3–19.

Gutman, J. 1982. "A Means-End Chain Model Based on Consumer Categorization Processes." *Journal of Marketing* 46, no. 2, pp. 60–72.

Gutman, J. 1997. "Means-Ends Chains as Goal Hierarchies." *Psychology and Marketing* 14, no. 6, pp. 545–60.

Thomas, J.R., and J. Gutman. 1988. "Laddering Theory, Method, Analysis, and Interpretation." *Journal of Advertising Research* 28, no. 3, pp. 11–31.

Hill, N., and J. Alexander. 2006. *Handbook of Customer Satisfaction and Loyalty Measurement*, 3rd ed. Aldershot, UK: Gower Technical Press.

Holbrook, M., and E. Hirschman. 1982. "The Experiential Aspects of Consumption: Consumer Fantasies, Feelings, and Fun." *Journal of Consumer Research* 9, pp. 132–40.

Houston, M.J. 1979. "Consumer Evaluations and Product Information Sources." In *Current Issues and Research in Advertising*, eds. J.H. Leigh, and C.R. Martin, 2 vols, pp. 135–44.

Hoyer, W.D., D.J. MacInnis, and R. Pieters.2012.*Consumer Behavior*, 6th ed. New York, NY: Houghton Mifflin.

Social Science Research Network, https://www.ssrn.com/en/.

Hutt, M.D., and T.W. Speh. 2003. *Business Marketing Management: A Strategic View of Industrial and Organizational Markets*. Mason, OH: South-Western College Publishing.

Johnson, D.S., J.M. Rogers, and L. Tan. 2001. "A Century of Family Budgets in the United States." *Monthly Labor Review* 124, pp. 28–45.

Jonathan, V., J.M. Lewis, and R.M. Kreider. 2013. *America's Families and Living Arrangements: 2012*. Washington, DC: U.S. Census Bureau, https://census.gov/prod/2013pubs/p20--570.pdf

Katona, G., and E. Mueller. 1955. "A Study of Purchase Decisions." In *Consumer Behavior: The Dynamics of Consumer Reactions*, ed. L.H. Clark, 30–87. New York, NY: New York University Press.

MacNeil, I.R. 1978. "Contracts: Adjustment of Long-Term Economic Relations Under Classical, Neoclassical, and Relational Contract Law." *Northwestern University Law Review* 72, pp. 854–905.

Likert, R. 1961. *New Patterns of Management*. New York, NY: McGraw-Hill.

Newman, J., and R. Staelin. August, 1972. "Prepurchase Information Seeking for New Cars and Major Household Appliances." *Journal of Marketing Research* 9, pp. 249–57.

Old Spice Commercial 2018. https://nerdist.com/dungeons-and-dragons-gentleman-class-old-spice/

Ormrod, J.E. 2015. *Human Learning*, 7th ed. Upper Saddle River, NJ: Prentice-Hall.

Ratneshwar, S., L.W. Barsalou, C. Pechmann, and M. Moore. 2001. "Goal-Derived Categories: The Role of Personal and Situational Goals in Category Representations." *Journal of Consumer Psychology* 10, no. 3, pp. 147–57.

Ratneshwar, S., D.G. Mick, and C. Huffman. 2003. *The Why of Consumption: Perspectives on Consumer Motives, Goals and Desires*. New York, NY: Routledge.

Reeve, J.M. 2004. *Understanding Motivation and Emotion*, 4th ed. New York, NY: Wiley.

Reilly, M., and R. Holman. 1977. "Does Task Complexity or Cue Intercorrelation Affect Choice of an Information Processing Strategy: An Empirical Investigation." *In Advances in Consumer Research*, ed. W.D. Perreault, 185–90. 4 vols. Chicago: Association for Consumer Research.

Richard, P. 2001. "Operators See Safety Net in Trade Downs." *Nation's Restaurant News*, April 16.

Runyon, K., and D.W. Stewart. 1987. *Consumer Behavior and the Practice of Marketing*. Columbus, OH: Merrill Publishing.

Schwarz, N., and L.A. Vaughn. 2002. "The Availability Heuristic Revisited: Ease of Recall and Content of Recall as Distinct Sources of Information." In *Heuristics and Biases: The Psychology of Intuitive Judgment*, eds. T. Gilovich, D. Griffin, and D. Kahneman. New York, NY: Cambridge University Press.

Sheth, J.N. 1973. "A Model of Industrial Buyer Behavior." *Journal of Marketing* 37, pp. 50–56.

Shugan, S.M. September, 1980. "The Cost of Thinking." *Journal of Consumer Research* 7, pp. 99–111.

Singer, M. 1971. "The Vitality of Mythical Numbers." *Public Interest* 23, no. 410.

Social Issues Research Centre. February 13, 2018. "Social and Cultural Aspect of Drinking." http://sirc.org/publik/drinking6.html

Sternberg, R.J. 2006. *Cognitive Psychology*, 4th ed. Belmont, CA: Thomson Wadsworth.

Stewart, D.W. 1989. "Measures, Methods, and Models of Advertising Response Over Time." *Journal of Advertising Research* 29, pp. 54–60.

Stewart, D.W., and M.A. Kamins. 1993. *Secondary Research, Information Sources and Methods*. Thousand Oaks, CA: Sage.

Strategic Business Insights 2018. "VALS," http://sric-bi.com/vals/

Swan, J.E., and L.J. Combs. April, 1976. "Product Performance and Consumer Satisfaction: A New Concept." *Journal of Marketing* 40, pp. 25–33.

Temporal, P. 2001. "Boon Rawd Brewery: Researching Beer Brand Image and Strategy Options." In *Branding in Asia: The Creation, Development, and Management of Asian Brands for the Global Market*, 170—80. New York, NY: John Wiley.

The U.S. Census Bureau provides up-to-date demographic information about the United States and links to information in other countries on its website at: http://census.gov/

Thomas, J.R., and J.C. Olson. 2001. *Understanding Consumer Decision Making: The Means-end Approach to Marketing and Advertising Strategy*. Mahwah, NJ: Erlbaum; Thorstein, V. 1899, Reprinted 2005. *The Theory of the Leisure Class*. New York, NY: Dodo Press.

Wagner, E.T. September 12, 2013. "Five Reasons 8 out of 10 Businesses Fail." *Forbes*. https://forbes.com/sites/ericwagner/2013/09/12/five-reasons-8-out-of-10-businesses-fail/#64079ac76978

Warland, R.H., R.O. Herman, and J. Williams. Summer, 1975. "Dissatisfied Consumers: Who Gets Upset and Who Takes Action." *Journal of Consumer Affairs* 9, pp. 104–15.

Webster, F.E., Jr., and Y. Wind. 1972. *Organizational Buying Behavior*. Englewood Cliffs, NJ: Prentice-Hall.

Wright, E.O. 2005. *Approaches to Class Analysis*. New York, NY: Cambridge University Press.

Yoram W., and T.S. Robertson. 1982. "The Linking Pin Role of the Organizational Buying Center." *Journal of Business Research* 10, pp. 169–84.

Young and Rubicam 2018. "Young and Rubicam's 4c's Theory." https://frameshortfilmjamie.wordpress.com/category/young-and-rubicam-4cs/; see also Issuu 2018. "The Are Seven Kinds of People in the World," https://issuu.com/youngandrubicam/docs/4cs

Zaichkowsky, J.L. December, 1985. "Measuring the Involvement Construct." *Journal of Consumer Research* 12, pp. 341–52.

About the Author

David W. Stewart, PhD is President's Professor of Marketing and Business Law at Loyola Marymount University, Los Angeles. He has previously held faculty and administrative appointments at Vanderbilt University, the University of Southern California, and the University of California, Riverside. Dr Stewart is a past editor of the *Journal of Marketing*, the *Journal of the Academy of Marketing Science,* and the *Journal of Public Policy and Marketing*. He is founding chair of the Marketing Accountability Standard Board (MASB). He currently serves as Vice President, Publications for the American Marketing Association and has served on the Board of Governors of the Academy of Marketing Science and as Vice President, Finance and a member of the Board of Directors of the American Marketing Association. He is a past-president of the Academic Council of the American Marketing Association, a past chairman of the Section on Statistics in Marketing of the American Statistical Association, a past president of the Society for Consumer Psychology, and a Fellow of both the American Psychological Association and the Association for Psychological Science. He has also previously served as a member and past-chairman of the United States Census Bureau's Advisory Committee of Professional Associations.

Dr Stewart has authored or coauthored more than 250 publications and 12 books. Dr Stewart's research has examined a wide range of issues including marketing strategy, the analysis of markets, consumer information search and decision making, effectiveness of marketing communications, public policy issues related to marketing, and methodological approaches to the analysis of marketing data. His research and commentary are frequently featured in the business and popular press. A native of Baton Rouge, Louisiana, Professor Stewart received his BA from the Northeast Louisiana University (now the University of Louisiana at Monroe) and his MA and PhD in psychology from Baylor University.

Dr Stewart is the recipient of the American Marketing Association's Award for Lifetime Contributions to Marketing and Public Policy, the Elsevier Distinguished Marketing Scholar Award from the Society for Marketing Advances and the Cutco/Vector Distinguished Educator Award by the Academy of Marketing Science. He has also received the American Academy of Advertising Award for Outstanding Contributions to Advertising Research for his long-term contributions to research in advertising.

Professor Stewart's experience includes work as a manager of research for Needham, Harper, and Steers Advertising, Chicago (now DDB) and consulting projects for a wide range of organizations. Among the organizations for which Dr Stewart has consulted are Hewlett Packard, Agilent Technologies, the Coca-Cola Company, Hughes, NCR, Texas Instruments, IBM, Intel, Cadence Design Systems, Century 21 Real Estate, Samsung, American Home Products, Visa Services, Xerox, the U.S. Census Bureau and the United States Federal Trade Commission, among others. He has served as an expert witness before the Federal Trade Commission, in United States Federal Court, and in State Courts in cases involving deceptive advertising claims and unfair business practices, in matters related to trademarks and intellectual property, and in anti-trust actions. Professor Stewart has delivered executive education programs throughout the United States and in more than 20 other nations on five continents. In 1988, he was Marketing Science Institute Visiting Scholar at the General Motors Corporation.

Index